MW00785363

A Day for a Lay

Also by Gavin Geoffrey Dillard:

In the Flesh—undressing for success
Between the Cracks
Yellow Snow (and other poems)
The Naked Poet
Pagan Love Songs
Waiting for the Virgin
Notes from a Marriage

(Gavin Dillard's archives are housed
in the James C Hormel Collection
of the Gay and Lesbian Center
at the San Francisco Library.)

A DAY FOR A LAY

a century of gay poetry

edited by

Gavin Geoffrey Dillard

BARRICADE BOOKS

New York City

1999

Published by Barricade Books, Inc.
150 Fifth Avenue, New York, NY 10003

Copyright © 1999 by GAVCO

All rights reserved. No part of this book may be reproduced in any form without permission in writing from the publisher, except by a reviewer, who may quote brief passages.

All poems are copyright by the author unless otherwise stated.
All poems are printed by permission of the author or copyright holder.
See *"Permissions"*—page 301.

Cover photo by Gavin Dillard.
Author photo by Jan E Watson.

First Edition

ISBN: 1-56980-134-7

dedicated to Harold Norse

*with additional thanks to Ian Young,
David Dalton, William Barrett
and Leonard Mae Robinson*

Contents

Introduction

The student of homosexual poetry may note a number of omissions in this text. They are deliberate. Not only have I left out some very famous poets—and I have included some rather obscure ones—but I also have selected, even from the most famous, only those pieces that I consider world class. Some are world class because they have survived the test of time. Others, I am convinced, solely from my own reckoning, are world class because they will go on to define our lives and our loves in the millennium to come.

Many of these poems—such as Ed Field's "Moving Man," Master Congdon's prose poem "Jagannath," and Takahashi's astonishing "Ode"—have haunted me for well over two decades. Such is the measure of fine art. This is the work that I have sought to recognize in this anthology, lest it be lost to us except in the lonely vaults of queer archives.

The book includes only poets who published during this century. The beloved 19th Century poets Rimbaud and Whitman are amply covered elsewhere. I have included—and borrowed for the title of this collection—the closeted Auden's surreptitiously-passed-around "A Day for a Lay." I am very happy to publish some of the once-buried poems by England's obscure but remarkably *un*closeted Ralph Chubb. Included is the famous "Two Loves" poem by Lord Alfred Douglas, Oscar Wilde's inconstant, though constantly loved, *Bosie*. And I am pleased to print new translations of Constantine Cavafy and of Genet's grueling "The One Condemned to Death."

And of course, to round out the anthology, I have included some new poems by young poets that are either extraordinary in their primal reality—Vytautas Pliura's heartbreaking "Thomas," for example—or poems that otherwise promise to be of lasting merit.

In most cases I have leaned toward intimacy versus politics. Intimacy is more authentic, more timeless, and bucks the masculinist agenda. Yet I have avoided, whenever possible, the oh-where-oh-where-is-my-true-love sentiment. Such sophomoric renderings are the country songs of verse. My focus has been narrative, as in David Bergman's gorgeous "The Blueberry Man," or his "A Part for Horn"—which made me weep upon first reading. It is the stories that we tell about ourselves that survive time and that illustrate to future generations who we were and who they might be.

I also have generally avoided the staunchly academic, that face-hiding gunny sack of erudition that is worn to avoid the spilling of one's soul, and I have opted instead for work that is raw yet contains elements so universal that it is the gut that reacts and not the mind. Nor has prestigious publication swayed me in my choices. Two of America's most famous bards, Whitman and Rod McKuen, were entirely self-published, and others, such as Dickinson, were published only posthumously.

What is presented here is a compilation of twenty-some years of research. I am eternally indebted to such preceding efforts as Ian Young's *Male Muse* series, the various *Gay Sunshine* anthologies, and the myriad periodicals, publications, and anthologies that have sprung up like blossoms in our glorious dance through time.

When I was in high school, at the North Carolina School of the Arts, I was asked to write a poem for an English class. The resulting poem caused my teacher, Alton Buzbee, a local poet, to pull me from high school English and spend the next two years tutoring me in poetry.

By and by Buzbee laid a handful of my poems on another local bard, Jonathan Williams, who in turn took them to England and handed them to Canadian poet Ian Young, who came back to the states and published my first two books of poetry. Such began my career as a poet. I was nineteen.

During those high school years, someone gave me a copy of Winston Leyland's *Gay Sunshine,* still the most important and well-edited publication of its kind, containing not only art, stories and poetry, but also interviews with Ginsberg, Burroughs, John Weiners, Ned Rorem, Harold Norse. Here at last I began to identify myself not only as a poet and an artist, but also as a homosexual poet and artist.

Shortly after this I began having work published in *Gay Sunshine,* in Andrew Bifrost's short-lived New York-based quarterly, *Mouth of the Dragon,* and eventually in Ian Young's second anthology of gay poetry, *The Son of the Male Muse.* I was now hobnobbing with and corresponding with Allen Ginsberg, Kirby Congdon, Felice Picano, and other icons of the poetry world. I had a career, an identity, and a society in which I at last did fit.

Now, many years later, as an editor, living within a reasonable drive of San Francisco, I have befriended the octogenarian Harold Norse—to whom I have dedicated this volume—a man whose discovery of and translation of the Italian poet GG Belli in the mid 1950s virtually ushered in the Beat scene, spading in the roots of what would evolve into "modern gay poetry."

Thus have been my encounters with the people that I consider the most influential in the development of our unique creative genre.

To my fellow students of the Muse, I say: We are not alone. We have never been alone. We belong to a family of muses. Though we have been blatantly or subtly disenfranchised at times, still we have survived the eons. Nor are we barren, as our detractors claim, for we have ceaselessly given birth to the muses of tomorrow.

Peace and poesy,
Gavin Geoffrey Dillard
Bolinas, California
January, 1999

A Day for a Lay

Edward Carpenter

(1844 – 1929)

A leading disciple of Walt Whitman, Edward Carpenter became an eloquent spokesman for libertarian socialism, feminism, Eastern Philosophy and homosexual liberation. His books, including The Intermediate Sex *and the poetry collection* Towards Democracy, *were written at his country cottage in Millthorpe, where he lived openly with his lover, George Merrill. An influential and widely respected figure, his reputation faded after his death, to be revived by the Gay Liberation movement in the 1970s.*

from **Towards Democracy**

Through the Long Night

You, proud curve-lipped youth, with brown sensitive face,
Why, suddenly, as you sat there on the grass, did you turn full upon me
    those twin black eyes of yours,
With gaze so absorbing so intense, I a strong man trembled and was
    faint?
Why in a moment between me and you in the full summer afternoon
    did Love sweep—leading after it in procession across the lawn and the
    flowers and under the waving trees huge dusky shadows of Death and
    the other world?
I know not.
Solemn and dewy-passionate, yet burning clear and steadfast at the last,
Through the long night those eyes of yours, dear, remain to me—
And I remain gazing into them.

from **A Mightier than Mammon**

The love of men for each other—so tender, heroic, constant;
That has come all down the ages, in every clime, in every nation,
Always so true, so well assured of itself, overleaping barriers of age, of
    rank, of distance,
Flag of the camp of Freedom;
The love of women for each other—so rapt, intense, so confiding-close,
    so burning-passionate,
To unheard deeds of sacrifice, of daring and devotion, prompting;
And (not less) the love of men for women, and of women for men—
    on a newer greater scale than it has hitherto been conceived;
Grand, free and equal—gracious yet ever incommensurable—
The soul of Comradeship glides in.

The young heir goes to inspect the works of one of his tenants;
[Once more the king's son loves the shepherd lad;]
In the shed the fireman is shovelling coal into the boiler furnace. He is
    neither specially handsome nor specially intelligent, yet when he
    turns, from under his dark lids rimmed with coal dust shoots
    something so human, so loving-near, it makes the other tremble.
They only speak a few words, and lo! underneath all the differences of
    class and speech, of muscle and manhood, their souls are knit
    together.

The Cinghalese cooly comes on board a merchant vessel at Colombo,
    every day for a week or more, to do some bits of cleaning.
He is a sweet-natured bright intelligent fellow of 21 or so. One of the
    engineers is decently kind and friendly with him—gives him a knife
    and one or two little presents;
But the Cinghalese gives his very soul to the engineer; and worships his
    white jacket and overalls as though they were the shining garment of
    a god.
He cannot rest; but implores to be taken on the voyage; and weeps
    bitterly when he learns that the ship must sail without him.
Ah! weep not, brown-bodied youth wandering lonely by the surf-
    ridden shore—as you watch your white friend's vessel gliding into
    the offing, under the sun and the sun-fringed clouds;
Out, far out to sea, with your friend whom you will never see again;
Weep not so heart-brokenly, for even your tears, gentle boy, poured
    now upon the barren sand are the prophecy of amity that shall be
    one day between all the races of the earth.

And here are two women, both doctors and mature in their profession, whose souls are knit in a curiously deep affection.

They share a practice in a large town, and live in the same house together, exchanging all that they command, of life and affection and experience;

And this continues for twenty-years—till the death of the elder one—after which the other ceases not to visit her grave, twice every week, till the time of her own last illness.

And this is of a poor lad born in the slums, who with aching lonely heart once walked the streets of London.

Many spoke to him because he was fair—asked him to come and have a drink, and so forth; but still it was no satisfaction to him; for they did not give him that which he needed.

Then one day he saw a face in which love dwelt. It was a man twice his own age, captain of a sailing vessel—a large free man, well acquainted with the world, capable and kindly.

And the moment the lad saw him his heart was given to him, and he could not rest but must needs follow the man up and down—yet daring not to speak to him, and the other knowing nothing of it all.

And this continued—till the time came for the man to go another voyage. Then he disappeared; and the youth, still not knowing who or whence he was, fell into worse misery and loneliness than ever, for a whole year.

Till at last one day—or one evening rather—to his great joy he saw his friend going into a public house. It was in a little street off Mile-end Road. He slipped in and sat beside him.

And the man spoke to him, and was kind, but nothing more. And presently, as the hour was getting late, got up and said Goodnight, and went out the door.

And the lad, suddenly seized with a panic fear that he might never see his friend again, hurried after him, and when they came to a quiet spot, ran up and seized him by the hand, and hardly knowing what he was doing fell on his knees on the pavement, and held him.

And the man at first thought this was a ruse or a mere conspiracy, but when he lifted the lad and looked in his face he understood, for he saw love written there. And he straightaway loved and received him.

And this is of a boy who sat in school.

The masters talked about Greek accidence and quadratic equations, and the boys talked about lobs and byes and bases and goals; but of that which was nearest to his heart no one said a word.

It was laughed at—or left unspoken.

Yet when the boy stood near some of his comrades in the cricket-field
or sat next them in school, he stocked and stammered, because of
some winged glorious thing which stood or sat between him and
them.

And again the laughter came, because he had forgotten what he was
doing; and he shrank into himself, and the walls round him grew, so
that he was pent and lonely like a prisoner.

Till one day to him weeping, Love full-grown, all-glorious, pure,
unashamed, unshackled, came like a god into his little cell, and swore
to break the barriers.

And when the boy through his tears asked him how he would so that,
Love answered not, but turning drew with his finger on the walls of
the cell.

And as he drew, lo! beneath his finger sprang all forms of beauty, an
endless host—outlines and colors of all that is, transfigured:

And, as he drew, the cell-walls widened—a new world rose—and folk
came trooping in to gaze,

And the barriers had vanished.

Wonderful, beautiful, the Soul that knits the Body's life passed in,
And the barriers had vanished.

Constantine Cavafy

(1863 – 1933)

*One of the most important modern Greek poets, Constantine Cavafy spent
most of his life in Alexandria, Egypt, where he worked as a civil servant.
His poignant, often philosophical poems of erotic encounters, Alexandrian life,
and Greek history remain popular and influential, both in the originals and
in a variety of English translations.
(All translations by Gavin Dillard, except where noted.)*

Picture of a Youth of Twenty-three
Painted by His Friend of the Same Age, an Amateur
(translated by Ian Young)

He studies it carefully now,
the painting he completed
yesterday noon.
He has painted him
in a coat of deep gray, unbuttoned,
no vest or tie,
a rose-coloured shirt open at the collar
to show the beauty of his chest and neck.
His hair falls over his right temple,
his beautiful hair
parted in the fashionable manner.
The sensuous feeling is there
that he wanted to portray
when he painted the eyes,
the lips...
That mouth, those lips
so made for consummation,
for choice love-making.

The Tobacco-Shop Window

They stood among many others
near the lighted window of a tobacco shop.
By chance their glances met
and timidly, haltingly,
expressed the illicit craving of their flesh.
Then a few tentative steps along the street,
until they smiled and discreetly nodded.

And after that the enclosed carriage,
the physical closeness of their bodies,
the joining of hands, the meeting of lips ...

At the Next Table

He must be barely twenty-two, and yet
I am certain that just so many years ago
I enjoyed that selfsame body.

No, it isn't merely inlovement,
I only entered the tavern a moment ago and I've
hardly had a thing to drink—
but I have enjoyed that very body.

And if I can't recall where—one lapse of memory proves nothing.

There, see, now that he has sat at the next table,
I'm familiar with every move that he makes—
and beneath his clothes, I can envision those
naked limbs that I have loved.

Their Beginning

The consummation of their deviant, sexual
delight complete, they arose from the mattress
and quickly dressed without speaking.

They left the house one at a time, furtively,
and as each walked uneasily up the street, it seemed as if
something about himself perhaps did betray
into what sort of bed he had fallen mere moments ago.

But for the life of the artist, look what's been gained—
tomorrow, the next day, or years hence, the powerful
verses will be composed that here had their beginning.

Two Young Men, 23 and 24 Years Old

He'd been sitting in the café since ten-thirty,
expecting his friend to arrive any minute.
Midnight came and went, and still he waited.
And now it was after one-thirty and the
café was almost empty.
He was tired of reading the newspapers like a
machine. Of his three sparse shillings
only one remained: all that waiting, he had
spent the other two on coffee and brandy.
He'd smoked every last cigarette.
And all the waiting had exhausted him;
all those hours alone had weighed heavily on his
mind about this wicked life that he was leading.

But when his friend at last arrived—
weariness, boredom, his thoughts all
vanished at once.

His buddy brought some unexpected news.
He had just won sixty pounds at the casino.

Their exquisite faces, their sublime youth,
the sensual love that each felt toward the other
were refreshed, enlivened, strengthened by the
sixty pounds just garnered at the gambling table.

And full of joy and vitality, feeling and expression
they went—not to the houses of their respectable families
(where they were no longer desired anyway)—

but to a familiar and especially favored house of
debauchery, where they asked for a bedroom and expensive
drinks, and they drank some more.

And when the expensive drinks were finished,
and since it was almost four in the morning,
they joyfully surrendered to love.

In the 25th Year of His Life

He goes regularly to the tavern
where they had met in the preceding month.
He's made inquiries, but they've been
unable to tell him anything specific.
From what they've said, he's gathered that the
young man he'd met was unknown to all,
one of the many shady young waifs who
frequent the place.
Still he goes to the tavern faithfully, each night,
and sits there watching the doorway,
watching the doorway to the point of exhaustion—
he may come walking in, tonight might be the night.

For almost three weeks he's done this,
his mind still sick with desire.
Those kisses have stayed on his mouth,
his very flesh suffers from lustful yearning.
The touch of the other's body is all over him;
he longs for that union again.

Of course he tries to act discreet,
but at times he loses all caring.
Besides, he knows full well what he's exposing himself to,
he has resigned to the prospect—it is likely that this
life he's chosen will end in a devastating scandal.

Before Time Alters Them

They were both deeply grieved at their separation.
They did not want it, it was circumstance.
An essential job obliged one to go far away—
New York or Canada. It's true that their
love wasn't as it had been, the attraction had
gradually waned, as lust's attraction is wont
to do. But they did not want to be separated.
It was circumstance—

         Or perhaps Destiny had
appeared as an artist, separating them now before
their feelings should fade altogether, before
Time had had its way with them; so that
each for the other will remain forever as
he had been, a handsome young man of 24.

Days of 1901

There was something that set him apart from others,
that despite his immoral behavior, and his
vast experiences with love,
despite the notable congruence between his
attitude and his age,
there happened to be moments—rare moments,
to be sure—when he gave the impression of a flesh
virtually untouched.

The beauty of his twenty-nine years,
so tested by sexual indulgences,
at moments strangely recalled a
young man who—rather awkwardly—surrenders his
virginal body to love for the very first time.

Days of 1903

I have never found them again—those things so
quickly lost...
the poetic eyes, the pallid face...
in the dark of the road...

I have never found them again—those so haphazardly met,
that I gave up so easily,
and much later in agony I craved.
The poetic eyes, the pallid face...

I never found those lips again.

In Despair

He has lost him completely.
And now he searches for his taste on the
lips of each new lover; in the embrace of
each new lover, he pretends that it is into
his arms that he is falling.

He's lost him completely, as if he had never existed.
He wanted, his lover had said, to save himself
from the forbidden, the sick sexual passion;
the forbidden, shameful sexual passion.
There was still time, he had said, to save himself.

He's lost him completely, as if he had never existed.
In his imaginings, in his fantasies,
he is ever seeking those lips in the lips of another;
he is longing to feel again the love that he has known.

Where I Lingered and Lay Upon The Beds

Whenever I went to the house of pleasure
I never hung out in the front rooms where they
politely celebrated the more accepted forms of love.

I went into the secret rooms
where I lingered and lay upon the beds.

I went into the secret rooms
that they are too ashamed to name.
Yet not shameful to me—for if they were
what kind of poet, what kind of an artist would I be?
I'd rather be an ascetic. Such would be more in keeping,
much more in keeping with my poetry,
than for me to seek pleasures in the commonplace rooms.

The Bandaged Shoulder

He said that he'd hurt himself on a wall
or that he'd fallen down.
But there was probably another reason
for the wounded, bandaged shoulder.

With a rather abrupt movement,
while reaching for a shelf to bring down some
photographs he wanted to view more closely,
the bandage came undone and the blood again ran.

I rebandaged the shoulder, though
taking my time; he was in no real pain,
and I enjoyed looking at the blood.
That blood was a part of my love.

After he had gone I found a blood-soaked rag in
front of his chair, left to be
tossed into the garbage,
which I brought straightway to my mouth
and held there for an endless amount of time—
the blood of love upon my lips.

In the Taverns

I wallow in the taverns
and in the brothels of Beirut.
I didn't want to stay
in Alexandria. Tamides left me;
he went off with the Governor's son to earn himself
a villa on the Nile, a mansion in the city.
It wouldn't be acceptable for me to stay in Alexandria—
I wallow in the taverns
and in the brothels of Beirut.
I live an abject life, devoted to cheap debauchery.
The only thing that saves me,
like immortal beauty, like a fragrance that
remains forever on my skin, is that I possessed Tamides
for two full years, the most exquisite of young men,
mine completely, and not for a house or a villa on the Nile!

Hidden Things

(translated by Gloria Brame and Gavin Dillard)

From everything that I have done and said
let no one try to understand me.
There was an obstacle which distorted
the actions and the style of my life.
An obstacle was there to
silence me when I wanted to speak.
From my least-known actions and my most cryptic poems—
from these alone will I be understood.
But perhaps it isn't worth my concern and my effort
that they might someday discover who I really am.
For later, in a more perfect society,
some other fellow who is created like me
most surely will appear and act freely.

Lord Alfred Douglas

(1870 – 1945)

Forever notorious as the lover who goaded Oscar Wilde into court, Lord Alfred Douglas was an accomplished minor poet; it was he who coined the phrase "the love that dare not speak its name." During the long years after Wilde's death, the waspish Douglas vacillated erratically between championing his old friend and vilifying him.

Two Loves

Two loves I have of comfort and despair
    Which like two spirits do suggest me still,
The better angel is a man right fair,
    The worser spirit a woman coloured ill.

—*Shakespeare*

I dreamed I stood upon a little hill,
And at my feet there lay a ground, that seemed
Like a waste garden, flowering at its will
With flowers and blossoms. There were pools that dreamed
Black and unruffled; there were white lilies
A few, and crocuses, and violets
Purple or pale, snake-like fritillaries
Scarce seen for the rank grass, and through green nets
Blue eyes of shy pervenche winked in the sun.
And there were curious flowers, before unknown,
Flowers that were stained with moonlight, or with shades
Of Nature's wilful moods; and here a one
That had drunk in the transitory tone
Of one brief moment in a sunset; blades
Of grass that in an hundred springs had been
Slowly but exquisitely nurtured by the stars,
And watered with the scented dew long cupped
In lilies, that for rays of sun had seen

Only God's Glory, for never a sunrise mars
The luminous air of heaven. Beyond, abrupt,
A gray stone wall, o'ergrown with velvet moss,
Uprose. And gazing I stood long, all mazed
To see a place so strange, so sweet, so fair.
And as I stood and marvelled, lo! across
The garden came a youth, one hand he raised
To shield him from the sun, his wind-tossed hair
Was twined with flowers, and in his hand he bore
A purple bunch of bursting grapes, his eyes
Were clear as crystal, naked all was he,
White as the snow on pathless mountains frore,
Red were his lips as red wine-spilth that dyes
A marble floor, his brow chalcedony.
And he came near me, with his lips uncurled
And kind, and caught my hand and kissed my mouth,
And gave me grapes to eat, and said 'Sweet friend,
Come, I will shew thee shadows of the world
And images of life. See, from the south
Comes the pale pageant that hath never an end.'
And lo! within the garden of my dream
I saw two walking on a shining plain
Of golden light. The one did joyous seem
And fair and blooming, and a sweet refrain
Came from his lips; he sang of pretty maids
And joyous love of comely girl and boy,
His eyes were bright, and 'mid the dancing blades
Of golden grass his feet did trip for joy.
And in his hands he held an ivory lute,
With strings of gold that were as maidens' hair,
And sang with voice as tuneful as a flute,
And round his neck three chains of roses were.
But he that was his comrade walked aside;
He was full sad and sweet, and his large eyes
Were strange with wondrous brightness, staring wide
With gazing; and he sighed with many sighs
That moved me, and his cheeks were wan and white
Like pallid lilies, and his lips were red
Like poppies, and his hands he clenchèd tight,
And yet again unclenchèd, and his head
Was wreathed with moon-flowers pale as lips of death.
A purple robe he wore, o'erwrought in gold
With the device of a great snake, whose breath

Was fiery flame: which when I did behold
I fell a-weeping and I cried, 'Sweet youth,
Tell me why, sad and sighing, thou dost rove
These pleasant realms? I pray thee speak me sooth
What is thy name?' He said, 'My name is Love.'
Then straight the first did turn himself to me
And cried, 'He lieth, for his name is Shame,
But I am Love, and I was wont to be
Alone in this fair garden, till he came
Unasked by night; I am true Love, I fill
The hearts of boy and girl with mutual flame.'
Then sighing said the other, 'Have thy will,
I am the Love that dare not speak its name.'

In Praise of Shame

Unto my bed last night, methought there came
Our lady of strange dreams, and from an urn
She poured live fire, so that mine eyes did burn
At sight of it. Anon the floating flame
Took many shapes, and one cried, 'I am Shame
That walks with Love, I am most wise to turn
Cold lips and limbs to fire; therefore discern
And see my loveliness, and praise my name.'

And afterward, in radiant garments dressed,
With sound of flutes and laughing and glad lips,
A pomp of all the passions passed along,
All the night through; till the white phantom ships
Of dawn sailed in. Whereat I said this song,
'Of all sweet passions Shame is loveliest.'

Ralph Chubb

(1892 – 1960)

*A reclusive visionary who produced his own books in limited editions on a
private printing press in the English countryside, Ralph Chubb was of the
generation who fought in, and were deeply troubled by, the carnage of
World War I. His magnificently illustrated volumes, influenced by Blake,
emphasize adolescent eros as part of a magic kingdom, infused with a
Whitmanesque religion of beauty and peace.*

Boys on the Quay

With dockside urchins on the quay
Piping husky shouts of glee
I pad the street with happy feet
Mischievous and wild and free.
The pavement reeks with dust and heat;
It is a summer holiday:
We watch the labourors—they sweat;
We laugh and scamper off in play!
We lean o'er railings at our ease,
and mock the citizens and tease,
And joke and smoke and spit and swear.
The hum of noon is in the air,
The sun is dancing on the wave,
Which laps against the timber pier
And echoes from the distant cave.
A steamer's siren hoots and dies,
Sultry and still the harbor lies,
The tide is filling to the brim,
'Tis time we boys should have a swim.
Out of our dirty rags we slip,
And mother-naked run and skip,
While thirsty passers pause and stare
To see us play stark-naked there
And cool our bodies in the breeze
And play rude gambols as we please.

Some look with pleasure, some disgust,
Or with indifference, or lust;
While we crack jests among ourselves,
For impudence, like saucy elves!
We swim and frolic in the sea,
And duck and dive and sport and leap,
Like little tritons of the deep,
Happy, freest of the free,
Heedless of the decent sheep—
Who so fetterless as we?

from **The Book of God's Madness,** Part 3

Liveliest effigy of the human race,
Loveliest in form, in spirit like a sword,
Boyhood! I weep to see you so disgraced,
From stream's and meadow's playground snatched away
To die on commerce' bloody altar-stone.
I weep for you alone; none cares beside.
What sort of love is that that loves you best
When you are least yourself? I love in you
The very wantonness which others hate.
I love the wilful animal in you;
Your wayward wickedness is my delight.
I love you as I love the squirrel wild,
The wild wood-dove the gruesome sportsman murders,
The nightingale they slay to eat his tongue,
The playful seal, whose coat their females filch.
Youth, who of human kind can sing most sweet,
You dare not lift your voice for fear of scorn,
Because you know not friends from enemies.
There is an art in disobedience.
Rescue yourself, then save your sister dear,
Weaker than you, that ghouls have quite enslaved.
Ye ghouls, who worship mediocrity,
You clothe the beauteous flesh in ugliness,
Yourselves all paunch and rump from evil living
(Call it good living, wink, and all agree)
Turn you God's image to indecency?

Delicious form of youth I love your view,
Your feel, your sound, your scent, your taste, your all—
Your head, with crumpled hair, smooth cheeks and chin,
Soft lips and ears and nostrils, glowing eyes,
Lashes and eyebrows, throat and nape of neck,
Shoulders and armpits savoury with sweat,
Broad breasts with nipples, arms and wrists and hands,
Belly and navel, back and shoulder blades,
Caressing shapely buttocks, groins and hips,
Genitals dangling in a cluster down,
Thick thighs and knees, shins, ankles, calves and feet.
I speak to woman. —Here behold your king!
Lovelier than you, let flattering fools deny!
Mark his high glance, the swords of flickering light
That play about his shapely eager brow!
Whatever you have he has fuller store
Of good and bad, in flesh and spirit both.
In kind the same you are, in measure less—
Save in your *difference*. Glorious mother, how
My heart melts in your heart of ruddy flame!
The love of man and youth is as two fires,
Of mother and son two strong and gentle streams,
The love of man and maid a sluggish rill.
O! my mind swims; all images resolve
In dancing specks. Athwart a motley crew
Surges and glimmers; now a goodly youth,
Naked, triumphant, spurning with his foot
A heap of lumber, shattered instruments,
Books, broken statues, tumbled palaces;
And women, babes and elder men
Bowing before him and all crying out,
'Worthiest full life who fullest life enjoys!'
And he made answer on high, 'Is any here
Of fuller being than I? I'll bow to him!'

Song of My Soul

The form of youth without blemish, is not such the form divine?
Children of love, today I will sing my song to you!

Under the sky in the hot noon-beam, in the water-meadow,
The sound of the rushing fall;
We two alone together screen'd by the trees and the thicket;
Naked the lecherous urchin, the slim beautiful boy,
Naked myself, dark, muscled like a god, the hardy enduring man;
He a fully form'd human being in his way,
Myself a fully form'd human being in my way;
No patronage between us, mutual respect, two equal persons;
He knowing the universe, I knowing the universe, equal together;
I having every whit as much to learn from him as he from me;
From him to me, from me to him, reciprocal sexual spiritual love.

No word needed, scarce ev'n a glance, mystically
Limbs interlace, bodies interpenetrate,
Spirits coalesce.
(He scarce needs to be there, 'tis in Imagination's realm true lovers meet.)
O burning tongue and hot lips of me exploring my love!
Lave his throat with the bubbling fountain of my verse!
Drench him! Slake his loins with it, most eloquent!
Leave no part, no crevice unexplored; delve deep, my minstrel tongue!
Let our juices flood and mingle! Let the prophetic lava flow!
Drink deep of love, the pair of us, O sacramental communion,
As our souls meet and melt!
The sweat of our armpits runneth down upon our breasts.
Be our bodies sealèd together, part they with a smack!
I will be father and mother at once to thee, my son, thou shalt feed
    from my bosom.
And you shall be mother and father to me, and give me to suck my
    honey'd inspiration from your right nipple and from your left.
You shall leave no portion of me untasted, I will become fluid for your
    sake.
I will feed you spiritually with a stuff that shall make a man of you.
With the milk of divine manhood will I satisfy your soul.
Quick, your lips under my poetic dug,
My own soul's calf, pull, pull. Well out the manly hymns!
For I am he that shall fill your young veins with the seeds of all
    futurity.

from **The Sun Spirit**

At the time of puberty I had obsessions.

I walk'd always with downcast eyes and blush'd scarlet to meet anyone
in the street.

I thought I harbour'd a secret vice which none had discover'd before me.

I caught sight of my figure distorted in a shop window and thereafter
imagined that I had a physical deformity which others ignored
through kindness.

I believed that I stank.

If one raised his handkerchief to his nose even across the road I thought
it was to shut off my noisesomeness.

The schoolmaster with whom I had most to do was an ignorant self-
complacent tyrant. He did me great wrongs.

No one understood me. None explained to me nor relieved me.

All shunned me. I suffered in silence, alone.

As a babe I came forth from the womb and sucked at my mother's
breast with gurgling and deep satisfied sighs.

As an infant wee my fingers sought to my flesh unconscious happy.

Lying in my cot I caressed myself with innocent imaginings.

When I was now eight years old I went to the sea coast where I beheld
the village boys romp and paddle in stark nakedness upon the
beach.

Their forms were white and smooth like lilies.

My young heart ached with longing.

At about twelve years old I began to feel my sex.

One night on going to bed I stripped my skin bare before the glass and
surveyed my parts in different attitudes back and front.

Behold I appeared lovely and I thanked heaven that I was a boy.

I straddled the rocking-horse with my fork I squeezed harder and
harder upon the cushion-pad.

My face flashed my eyes sparkled. My heart beat faster faster,

Thrills passed through me. I had a movement of ecstasy.

  Suddenly a chill of disgust came over me.

Revolted at myself I got into my nightshirt and slunk ashamèd into bed.

My father came in the room to me with anxious face and said, What
have you been doing little son? What have you been doing?

I replied, Nothing, papa, and he went away anxious.

I became surly nervous reticent by day, rejoicing in solitude by night, a
butt for my school fellows, hearing them hint, from their
knowledge at what I understood not, longing for explanation
but kept out.

My lustful imaginings ran wild, I took part in orgies of phantasy.
Certain of my mates I loved passionately for their wayward beauty and
    yearn'd in secret for their caresses, but they rebuff'd me.
At night our invisible bodies met towselling in unlicensed intercourse.
As yet I knew nothing of the business of parenthood.
Nobody inform'd me. I long'd for relief, but none was vouchsafed me.
At eighteen years one Sunday in the mighty vaulted church I caught
    the glance of a dark-eyed chorister.
Instantly our souls flew to meet each other in wild embrace.
Had we not loved since the beginning with deepest love for ever and
    ever?
Such was the awakening of my spring. My eyes were open'd to love.
My friends perceived it and felt for me.
At this time I was exceedingly comely in both face and form and most
    happy and free from care.
My friends delighted in me and I in them.
We lay abed bestowing close kisses of comradeship.
Then providence fulfilled my desire and gave me as a lover a youth of
    fifteen years.
Idling we pass'd our sunny days bathing in sequester'd streams,
Sprawling with gold-brown bodies side-by-side beneath the noonday
    beam,
Fondling, spending, silently embracing.
The mounting heart, the shorten'd breath, the surging onslaught of
    desire,
Sweet pulsing short-lived agony seeking relief, the brimming
    consolation and flood,
The drooping languor, the heavenly listless content with bright
    swimming pupils gazing up seraphical at the azure vault...

Wilfred Owen

(1893 – 1918)

Wilfred Owen was a brilliant, romantic young poet who found his voice while serving as an officer in World War I. Influenced by Keats and by his friend and fellow war poet Siegfried Sassoon, Owen responded to the pressure and horror of combat with some of the most moving war poetry ever written, much of it expressing anger and pity at the mass slaughter of young men, including many of his friends. He was killed one week before an armistice was declared.

To Eros

In that I loved you, Love, I worshipped you.
In that I worshipped well, I sacrificed.
All of most worth I bound and burnt and slew:
Old peaceful lives; frail flowers; firm friends; and Christ.

I slew all false loves; I slew all true,
That I might nothing love but your truth, Boy.
Fair fame I cast away as bridegrooms do
Their wedding garments in their haste of joy.

But when I fell upon your sandalled feet,
You laughed; you loosed away my lips; you rose.
I heard the singing of your wings' retreat;
Far-flown, I watched you flush the Olympian snows,
Beyond my hoping. Starkly I returned
To stare upon the ash of all I burned.

Storm

His face was charged with beauty as a cloud
   With glimmering lightning. When it shadowed me
   I shook, and was uneasy as a tree
That draws the brilliant danger, tremulous, bowed.

So must I tempt that face to loose its lightning.
   Great gods, whose beauty is death, will laugh above,
   Who made his beauty lovelier than love.
I shall be bright with their unearthly brightening.

And happier were it if my sap consume;
Glorious will shine the opening of my heart;
The land shall freshen that was under gloom;
What matter if all men cry aloud and start,
And women hide bleak faces in their shawl,
At those hilarious thunders of my fall?

October, 1916

Sonnet to My Friend (with an Identity Disc)

If ever I had dreamed of my dead name
   High in the heart of London, unsurpassed
By Time for ever, and the Fugitive, Fame,
   There seeking a long sanctuary at last,—

Or if I onetime hoped to hide its shame,
   —Shame of success, and sorrow of defeats,—
Under those holy cypresses, the same
   That shade always the quiet place of Keats,

Now rather thank I God there is no risk
   Of gravers scoring it with florid screed.
Let my inscription be this soldier's disc...
   Wear it, sweet friend. Inscribe no date nor deed.
But may thy heart-beat kiss it, night and day,
Until the name grow blurred and fade away.

Maundy Thursday

Between the brown hands of a server-lad
The silver cross was offered to be kissed.
The men came up, lugubrious, but not sad,
And knelt reluctantly, half-prejudiced.
(And kissing, kissed the emblem of the creed.)
Then mourning women knelt; meek mouths they had,
(And kissed the Body of the Christ indeed.)
Young children came, with eager lips and glad.
(These kissed a silver doll, immensely bright.)
Then I, too, knelt before that acolyte.
Above the crucifix I bent my head:
The Christ was thin, and cold, and very dead:
And yet I bowed, yea, kissed—my lips did cling
(I kissed the warm live hand that held the thing.)

Federico García Lorca

(1898 – 1936)

Born in the province of Granada, García Lorca is considered Spain's leading lyric poet and dramatist. His work is infused with his love of Granada's Arabic and Gypsy cultures. Conservative Spain was not conducive to open writing on homosexual themes, and many of Lorca's works remain incomplete, or have been destroyed or suppressed. He was executed by Fascist assassins at the beginning of the Spanish Civil War. (Translated by Greg Simon and Steven F White.)

Ode to Walt Whitman

By the East River and the Bronx
boys were singing, exposing their waists,
with the wheel, with oil, leather, and the hammer.
Ninety thousand miners taking silver from the rocks
and children drawing stairs and perspectives.

But none of them could sleep,
none of them wanted to be the river,
none of them loved the huge leaves
or the shoreline's blue tongue.

By the East River at Queensboro
boys were battling with industry
and the Jews sold to the river faun
roses of circumcision,
and over bridges and rooftops, the mouth of the sky emptied
herds of bison driven by the wind.

But none of them paused,
none of them wanted to be a cloud,
none of them looked for ferns
or the yellow wheel of the tambourine.

As soon as the moon rises
the pulleys will spin to alter the sky;

a border of needles will besiege memory
and the hearses will bear away those who don't work.

New York, mire,
New York, wire and death.
What angel is hidden in your cheek?
Whose perfect voice will sing the truths of wheat?
Who, the terrible dream of your bruised anemones?

Not for a moment, Walt Whitman, lovely old man,
have I failed to see your beard full of butterflies,
nor your corduroy shoulders frayed by the moon,
nor your thighs as pure as Apollo's,
nor your voice like a column of ash;
old man, beautiful as the mist,
you moaned like a bird
whose sex was pierced by a needle.
Enemy of the satyr,
enemy of the vine,
and lover of bodies beneath the rough blanket...

Not for a moment, virile beauty,
who among mountains of coal, billboards and railroads,
dreamed of becoming a river and sleeping like a river
with that comrade who would place in your breast
the small ache of an ignorant leopard.

Not for a moment, Adam of blood, Macho,
man alone at sea, Walt Whitman, lovely old man,
because on penthouse roofs,
gathered at bars,
emerging in waves from the sewers,
trembling between the thighs of chauffeurs,
or spinning on dance floors wet with absinthe,
the faggots, Walt Whitman, point you out.

He's one, too! That's right! And they land
on your luminous chaste beard,
blondes from the north, blacks from the sands,
crowds of howls and gestures,
like cats or like snakes,

the faggots, Walt Whitman, the faggots,
clouded with tears, flesh for the whip,
the boot, or the teeth of the lion tamers.

He's one, too! That's right! Stained fingers
point to the shore of your dream
when a friend eats your apple
with a slight taste of gasoline
and the sun sings in the navels
of boys who play under bridges.

But you didn't look for scratched eyes,
nor the darkest swamp where someone submerges children,
nor frozen saliva,
nor the curves slit open like a toad's belly
that the faggots wear in cars and on terraces
while the moon lashes them on the street corners of terror.

You looked for a naked body like a river.
Bull and dream who would join wheel with seaweed,
father of your agony, camellia of your death,
who would groan in the blaze of your hidden equator.

Because it's all right if a man doesn't look for his delight
in tomorrow morning's jungle of blood.
The sky has shores where life is avoided
and there are bodies that shouldn't reveal themselves in the dawn.

Agony, agony, dream, ferment and dream.
This is the world, my friend, agony, agony.
Bodies decompose beneath the city clocks,
war passes by in tears, followed by a million gray rats,
the rich give their mistresses
little illuminated dying things,
and life is neither noble, nor good, nor sacred.

Man is able, if he wishes, to guide his desire
through the veins of coral or a heavenly naked body.
Tomorrow, loves will become stones, and Time
a breeze that drowses in the branches.

That's why I don't raise my voice, old Walt Whitman,
against the little boy who writes
the name of a girl on his pillow,
nor against the boy who dresses as a bride
in the darkness of his closet,
nor against the solitary men in casinos
who drink prostitution's water with revulsion,
nor against the men with that green look in their eyes
who love other men and whose lips burn in silence.

But yes against you, urban faggots,
tumescent flesh and unclean thoughts.
Mothers of mud. Harpies. Sleepless enemies
of the love that bestows crowns of joy.

Always against you, who give boys
drops of foul death with bitter poison..
Always against you,
Fairies of North America,
Pájaros of Havana,
Jotos of Mexico,
Sarasas of Cádiz,
Apios of Seville,
Cancos of Madrid,
Floras of Alicante,
Adelaidas of Portugal.

Faggots of the world, murderers of the dove!
Slaves of women. Their bedroom bitches.
Opening in public squares like feverish fans
or ambushed in rigid hemlock landscapes.

No quarter given! Death
spills from your eyes
and gathers gray flowers at the mire's edge.
No quarter given! Attention!
Let the confused, the pure,
the classical, the celebrated, the supplicants
close the doors of the bacchanal to you.

And you, lovely Walt Whitman, stay asleep on the Hudson's banks
with your beard toward the pole, openhanded.

Soft clay or snow, your tongue calls for
comrades to keep watch over your unbodied gazelle.

Sleep on, nothing remains.
Dancing walls stir the prairies
and America drowns itself in machinery and lament.
I want the powerful air from the deepest night
to blow away flowers and inscriptions from the arch where you sleep,
and a black child to inform the gold-craving whites
that the kingdom of grain has arrived.

Luis Cernuda

(1903 – 1963)

Born in Seville, Luis Cernuda was one of the "Generation of 1927," and is now recognized as one of the most important Spanish poets. He expressed his homosexuality obliquely in his early, surrealist writings, and more directly in his later work. A natural rebel and outsider, he went into exile after the Spanish Civil War and died in Mexico. (Translated by Mañuel Ruiz.)

Birds of the Night

The French government—or was it the English?—placed a
plaque on the house at 8 Great College Street, Camden Town, London,
where a peculiar couple named Rimbaud and Verlaine had a
room, resided, drank, worked, and fucked for a handful of stormy
weeks. The ambassador and the mayor of course both attended the
dedication, along with all the other important folk who had
scorned Verlaine and Rimbaud while they were alive.

The house, like the surrounding neighborhood, is dark and grim—
the sordid grimness that accompanies poverty, not the funereal
grimness of spiritual riches.
When nighttime falls, a hand organ sounds from the sidewalk outside,
as it did in their time, echoing in the heavy gray air,
and the neighbors, just home from work, begin
dancing their way to the nearest pub.

It was a brief acquaintanceship shared between Verlaine the Drunkard
and Rimbaud the Unfathomable, brief and riddled with conflict.
Still, we can assume that it had its rewarding moments, if only in
the knowledge that one had liberated himself from an insufferable
mother, and the other from a tedious wife.
Freedom in this world, however, is never free, and they who had
escaped were doomed to pay a heinous price.

As the plaque confirms, the two lived behind these walls, prisoners
of their destinies—an impossible friendship, the bitterness of

separation, the ensuing scandal; for the one, the trial and
two years in jail for conduct that society and its laws condemn,
at least at the time, and for the other, solitary wandering from
one obscure corner of the earth to another, always in
flight from the world and its vainglorious progress.

The pensive silence of the one, and the common yammering of the
other balanced out. Rimbaud fought off the oppressive hand while
Verlaine kissed it, accepting his due punishment. One hoarded his
gold in his belt, the other squandered his in absinthe and
loose women; both were hounded by the authorities and
scorned by the good folk who grow fat from the efforts of others.
Even the Negro whore had the right to insult them.

But with the passing of time, their drunkenness and sodomy,
their scandalous poetry, their wayward and disorderly lives—
none of these matter anymore, and France uses both names and
their works for the glory of France and her ordered art.
Scholars retrace their acts and measure their footsteps, bringing
even the most intimate nuances of their lives to light.
Nobody is afraid of them anymore; nobody condemns.

'Verlaine? Oh, he was some smooth operator when it came to
la femme, just a regular dude like you or me. And Rimbaud? Why he
was as good a Catholic as any.' They quote fragments of *Le Bateau
Ivre* and read the sonnet about the vowels—but they skip
Verlaine because he's no longer fashionable, unlike Rimbaud whose
deluxe editions with their dubious texts get poured over and
discussed by junior poets from provinces all over the world.

Do the dead hear what the living say about them? Let us hope not!
Eternal silence must be something like a balm for those, like
Rimbaud and Verlaine, who lived by the word and died by the word.
But can the silence of the hereafter blot out the ludicrous and
repugnant palter of the here and now?
          Someone once desired that mankind had a single head,
to chop it off with one fell blow.
But in that wish he gave it more importance than it deserves:
better if it were a cockroach, simply to squash it.

Sandro Penna

(1906 – 1977)

A poet of Rome and its street-boys, Penna was helped and championed by the older Umberto Saba and the younger Pier Paoli Pasolini. Penna never strayed from his favorite subject, saying "I don't know how to write about anything else. Everything else is boring." (Translated by Ian Young and Marsha Jill Shakley.)

It is enough, loving boys,
to feel how their stillness
holds the sun in the hot sand.

It is always so. No strong wind comes
to move that blinding calm.

At evening, in the shadow of the cathedral,
with cries and cries the boys play.
But from the silence also tolls

the voice of useless bells.

You descend the black stairs of my tavern
all soaked with wind,
your beautiful hair fallen over
bright eyes in my distant heaven.

In the tavern smoke, the lingering
smell of harbour wind—
wind shaping the body and moving
toward the white sailors.

Here the dear city
where the high night does not disturb.
Solitary friends who pass and give
you a look of love. Oh, believe it...

Still it is sweet to find yourself
on an unknown road,
a boy in overalls
passing near you.

Gazing at the tired bicycle
he rests beside him,
you think, from where you are,
about his life, the home he goes to.

Still you remain on the unknown,
infinite road,
not wondering if your life
will stay as it is now.

In a dingy theatre pit
I found my angel.
He was smoking a cigarette
and his eyes were shining.

The sky is empty. But in the dark eyes
of a boy I shall seek my heaven.

Yet my god rides off on a bicycle
or casually pisses against a wall.

Unsteady my peace under the April sky,
green lights moving under the wind
by whim. Even the waters sleep,
their eyes open.

Boys run on the lawn and the wind
scatters them. From my heart
a single lightning flash of youth
fixes their white shirts, bright against the grass.

The insomnia of the swallows. The quiet
friend to greet me at the station.

To sit at an unknown table.
To sleep in a bed not my own.
To feel the deserted square
salute in a loving farewell.

My boy is light and nimble
as an April wind, and as quick to change.
But the grass is hot in my meadows. In vain
it begs for a more constant caress.

When the light weeps on the street
I would like to embrace a boy in silence.

When my boy appears at the inn
men smile at him, caught suddenly by light.
The parting, though, comes soon enough.
Remain unsettled and alone
between my thick hands, my angel.

A boy ran after a train.
He shouted to me: life won't wait!
Laughing, I saluted him
and startled into calm, walked away.

Sadness of love, where the boy's
white smile lingers
like a last seagull in the storm.

WH Auden

(1907 – 1973)

Considered one of the most important poets of the century, Wystan Hugh Auden came to prominence as the most brilliant of a group of left-wing English writers now known as "the Auden generation." He emigrated to the U.S. in 1939, where he met his companion and literary collaborator Chester Kallman. Many of his later poems deal with existential and religious matters. "Platonic Blow" (also known as "A Day for a Lay") was one of a number of erotic verses he circulated anonymously.

A Day for a Lay

It was a Spring day, a day for a lay, when the air
Smelled like a locker-room, a day to blow or get blown;
Returning from lunch I turned my corner and there
On a near-by stoop I saw him standing alone.

I glanced as I advanced. The clean white T-shirt outlined
a forceful torso; the light-blue denims divulged
Much. I observed the snug curves where they hugged the behind,
I watched the crotch where the cloth intriguingly bulged.

Our eyes met. I felt sick. My knees turned weak.
I couldn't move. I didn't know what to say.
In a blur I heard words, myself like a stranger speak
"Will you come to my room?" Then a husky voice, "o.k."

I produced some beer and we talked. Like a little boy
He told me his story. Present address: next door.
Half Polish, half Irish. The youngest. From Illinois.
Profession: mechanic. Name: Bud. Age: twenty-four.

He put down his glass and stretched his bare arm along
The back of my sofa. The afternoon sunlight struck
The blond hairs on the wrist near my head. His chin was strong,
His mouth sucky. I could hardly believe my luck.

And here he was, sitting beside me, legs apart.
I could bear it no longer. I touched the inside of his thigh.
His reply was to move it closer. I trembled, my heart
Thumped and jumped as my fingers went to his fly.

I opened a gap in the flap. I went in there.
I sought for a slit in the gripper shorts that had charge
Of the basket I asked for. I came to warm flesh, then to hair.
I went on. I found what I hoped. I groped. It was large.

He responded to my fondling in a charming, disarming way:
Without a word he unbuckled his belt while I felt,
And lolled back, stretching his legs. His pants fell away.
Carefully drawing it out, I beheld what I held.

The circumcised head was a work of mastercraft
With perfectly beveled rim, of unusual weight
And the friendliest red. Even relaxed, the shaft
Was of noble dimensions with the wrinkles that indicate

Singular powers of extension. For a second or two
It lay there inert, then it suddenly stirred in my hand,
Then paused as if frightened or doubtful of what to do
And then with a violent jerk began to expand.

By soundless bounds it extended and distended. By quick
Great leaps it rose, it flushed, it rushed to its full size,
Nearly nine inches long and three inches thick.
A royal column, ineffably solemn and wise.

I tested its length and strength with a manual squeeze,
I bunched my fingers and twirled them about the knob,
I stroked it from top to bottom. I got on my knees.
I lowered my head. I opened my mouth for the job.

But he pushed me gently away. He bent down. He unlaced
His shoes. He removed his socks. Stood up. Shed
His pants altogether. Muscles in arms and waist
Rippled as he whipped his T-shirt over his head.

I scanned his tan, enjoyed the contrast of brown
Trunk against white shorts taut around small

Hips. With a dig and a wriggle he peeled them down.
I tore off my clothes. He faced me, smiling. I saw all.

The gorgeous organ stood stiffly and straightly out
With a slight flare upwards. At each beat of his heart it threw
An odd little nod my way. From the slot of the spout
Exuded a drop of transparent viscous goo.

The lair of hair was fair, the grove of a young man,
A tangle of curls and whorls, luxuriant but couth.
Except for a spur of golden hairs that ran
To the neat navel, the rest of the belly was smooth.

Well-hung, slung from the fork of the muscular legs,
The firm vase of his sperm like a bulging pear,
Cradling its handsome glands, two Herculean eggs,
Swung as he came towards me, shameless, bare.

We aligned mouths. We entwined. All act was clutch,
All fact, contact, the attack and the interlock
Of tongues, the charms of arms. I shook at the touch
Of his fresh flesh, I rocked at the shock of his cock.

Straddling my legs a little I inserted his divine
Person between and closed on it tight as I could.
The upright warmth of his belly lay all along mine.
Nude, glued together, for a minute we stood.

I stroked the lobes of his ears, the back of his head
And the broad shoulders. I took bold hold of the compact
Globes of his bottom. We tottered. He fell on the bed.
Lips parted, eyes closed, he lay there, ripe for the act,

Mad to be had, to be felt and smelled. My lips
Explored the adorable masculine tits. My eyes
Assessed the chest. I caressed the athletic hips
And the slim limbs. I approved the grooves of the thighs.

I hugged, I snuggled into an armpit, I sniffed
The subtle whiff of its tuft, I lapped up the taste
Of its hot hollow. My fingers began to drift
On a trek of inspection, a leisurely tour of the waist.

Downward in narrowing circles they playfully strayed,
Encroached on his privates like poachers, approached the prick
But teasingly swerved, retreated from meeting. It betrayed
Its pleading need by a pretty imploring kick.

"Shall I rim you?" I whispered. He shifted his limbs in assent,
Turned on his side and opened his legs, let me pass
To the dark parts behind. I kissed as I went
The great thick cord that ran back from his balls to his ass.

Prying the buttocks aside, I nosed my way in
Down the shaggy slopes. I came to the puckered goal.
It was quick to my licking. He pressed his crotch to my chin.
His thighs squirmed as my tongue wormed in his hole.

His sensations yearned for consummation. He untucked
His legs and lay panting, hot as a teen-age boy,
Naked, enlarged, charged, aching to get sucked,
Clawing the sheet, all his pores open to joy.

I inspected his erection. I surveyed his parts with a stare
From scrotum level. Sighting along the underside
Of his cock I looked through the forest of pubic hair
To the range of the chest beyond, rising lofty and wide.

I admired the texture, the delicate wrinkles and the neat
Sutures of the capacious bag. I adored the grace
Of the male genitalia. I raised the delicious meat
Up to my mouth, brought the face of its hard-on to my face.

Slipping my lips around the Byzantine dome of its head
With the tip of my tongue I caressed the sensitive groove.
He thrilled to the trill. "That's lovely!" he hoarsely said,
"Go on! Go on!" Very slowly I started to move.

Gently, intently, I slid to the massive base
Of his tower of power, paused there a moment down
In the warm moist thicket, then began to retrace
Inch by inch the smooth way to the throbbing crown.

Indwelling excitements swelled at delights to come
As I descended and ascended those thick distending walls.

I grasped his root between left forefinger and thumb
And with my right hand tickled his heavy, voluminous balls.

I plunged with a rhythmical lunge, steady and slow
And at every stroke made a corkscrew roll with my tongue.
His soul reeled in the feeling. He whimpered "Oh!"
As I tongued and squeezed and rolled and tickled and swung.

Then I pressed on the spot where the groin is joined to the cock,
Slipped a finger into his arse and massaged him from inside.
The secret sluices of his juices began to unlock.
He melted into what he felt. "Oh Jesus!" he cried.

Waves of immeasurable pleasures mounted his member in quick
Spasms. I lay still in the notch of his crotch inhaling his sweat.
His ring convulsed round my finger. Into me, rich and thick,
His hot spunk spouted in gouts, spurted in jet after jet.

Jean Genet

(1910 – 1983)

*Like Villon in another century, Genet was a "poet of the gutters." A foundling and professional thief who spent years in juvenile institutions and prisons, he became a self-taught writer, best known for brilliant novels, plays and memoirs that combine psychological insight, poetic use of religious and street language, and perverse morality. His narrative lyrics fuse compassion for outsiders and outcasts with a fierce eroticism.
(Translated by Winston Tong, with assistance by Bruce Geduldig.)*

The One Condemned to Death

For Maurice Pilorge, a twenty-year-old murderer

The wind that rolls a heart upon the courtyard's stone,
An angel that sobs entangled in a tree,
The sky column that circumnavigates a marble sea
Throw emergency exits open in my night alone.

A starved bird that murders, the ashes' taste,
The souvenir on the wall of a slumbering eye,
And this wretched fist that threatens the sky
Draw into my palm your falling face.

This face much harder yet softer than what masks it
Weighs heavier in my hand than the stolen jewel
In that of the thief's, it is drowned in sorrow,
Somber and fierce, a bouquet greening the casket.

Your face is severe, that of a shepherd's, a Greek,
Trembling in the crux over which my hand closes,
With your dead female mouth and your eyes of roses,
And your archangel's nose as perhaps the beak.

What great evil melted into a spring
The glittering ice of a wicked decency,

That powdered your hair with stars clear and steely
And crowned you with thorns, so that your face would sing?

Tell me what mad misfortune had to shatter your sight
With a despair so intense that the savage pain grips
And adorns, in panic-stricken form, your oval lips,
Despite your chilling tears, with a smile of utter blight?

This evening do not croon *"Bullies of the Moon,"*
Rather, golden boy, become a princess in a tower
Dreaming forlornly of the poor love that was ours,
Or, be the blond messboy, on watch atop the pontoon.

Towards nightfall he descends to chant upon the deck
"Ave Maria Stella" to the seamen holding steady,
Kneeling and bareheaded, every sailor ready,
A swelling shaft in the hand of each roughneck.

And it's to stick the handle in you, adventurous young mate,
That these musclebound mariners tense up in their skivvies,
My lover, my lover, are you going to steal the keys
That'll unlock the sky for me where the mast vibrates?

From where do you reign and sow the white spell that covers
My page with these snows, in my prison so silent?
The dread of it, the dead amongst the flowers of violet,
Death to their cocks! Their phantom lovers!

On their feet of velour pass a prowling sentry,
In my sunken eyes rests the memory of you.
It's possible to evade them by escaping over the roof.
They say that Guyana is a torrid country.

O the sweetness of Devil's Island, impossibly distant,
O the sea and the palmtrees, Beauty's sky tent,
Transparent morns, foolish nights, calm evenings spent,
O all the skinheads and their flesh of satin!

Of some austere lover let's dream and indulge,
Huge as the Universe but blemished with shadows,
He'll strip us and strap us in these sinister shackles,
Between thighs of gold, upon his steaming bulge.

Chiseled from an angel, a dazzling bloke,
Worked up over nosegays of pinks and jasmine
In your luminous hands that bear them, trembling,
To his august flank, that your kisses provoke.

Sadness in my mouth! A swelling embitterment,
Swelling my poor heart! All my perfumed lovers
Leaving! In my broken voice I say: so long forever!
O balls so beloved and prick so insolent!

Hey kid, don't sing, drop your gypsy pose!
Become the girl with the neck, so pure and radiant,
Or if you're fearless be the melodic infant
Long dead in me before the axe's blows.

Child of honor so fair, crowned in lilacs
Lean over my bed, allowing my cock that mounts
To slap your gilded cheek. Your lover, he recounts,
Is your killer, with his task of a thousand whacks.

He sings that he once had your body and image,
And your heart, that never opened to the spur's pleas
From a massive cavalier. To have your round knees!
Your fresh neck, smooth hand, o brat to be your age!

To steal, to let fly your bloodstained paradise,
To paint a masterpiece with the dead who've gathered
Here in the hedges and there in the pastures,
The dead, dazed from arranging his teen heaven demise.

The solemn mornings, the rum, the cigarette,
Shadows of tobacco, of jail and sailors
Inspecting my cell, where the specter of a killer
Rolls me over and holds me with his heavy basket.

The song that traverses a world of grief
Is the cry of a pimp transfixed by your music,
The chant of a hanged man as rigid as a stick,
It's the enchanted call of an amorous thief.

For a lifebuoy a sleeper of sixteen cries and begs,
But not one mariner heeds the frantic call,

An infant stands upright, pinned against the wall,
Another sleeps locked down by his own knotted legs.

I have killed for the eyes of an indifferent beauty
Who never comprehended why my love's held back,
An unknown devotee on his gondola of black,
She's lovely as a ship and she dies adoring me.

When you are ready, armed for the kill,
Helmeted in blond hair, masked in violence,
During the insane and brief violins' cadence
Slash a landlady's throat, for your love of the thrill.

A chevalier of iron on earth will appear,
Impassive and cruel despite the era, visible
Through the imprecise movements of a weeping widow,
Don't tremble at all before his pale stare.

This apparition comes from the forbidden zone
Of crimes of passion. Child of profundities,
To be born from his body some astonishing potencies,
The perfumed discharge of his divine bone.

On the wool rug, a stone from the black mountain,
A hand on his hip, listen to him marching,
March towards the sun of his body, free of sinning,
And stretch, tranquil at the edge of his fountain.

Each festival of blood assigns a comely youth
To stand by the boy in his premiere trial.
Appease your fear and your latest denial.
Suck on my hard member like you suck an ice cube.

Tenderly gnaw at the prick that beats your cheek about,
Kiss my engorged shaft, thrust deep down your throat,
The total issue of my load, swallowed in one blow.
Strangle yourself with love, disgorge and do your pout.

Worship my tattooed torso, as a sacred totem woo
Unto the very point of tears, worship on bended knee
My rupturing sex that shoots you, better than artillery.
Worship this baton of mine that's going to penetrate you.

It leaps into your eyes, it swallows your soul,
Twist your head around a bit, and see it self-erect;
Perceiving how noble it'd be to kiss it from respect
You call it "Madam!" as you bow quite low.

Madam, we'll parish here, Madam listen to me,
The manor is haunted! the jail trembles and shakes.
Take us away together now, see how the earth quakes!
Let's fly to your room in Heaven, O Lady of Mercy!

Call up the sun, who'll cease my crying,
Strangle all those cocks! Snuff the executioner!
From behind my window pane the day grins like a loser.
Prison is a tasteless schoolroom to die in.

Upon my neck without hate, my neck unarmored,
Leave the indentations of your wolfish grin,
With your heart unmoved, graze on the tender skin
Beneath my collar, with the touch of a widow enamored.

O come my handsome sun, o come my night in Spain,
Arrive in my eyes, for tomorrow I die,
Arrive at my door, your hand in mine to fly
Far from here, together, to conquer our domain.

The heavens can awaken the stars to bloom,
The flowers to sigh as meadows of black grass
Receiving morning dew, as a drink in a glass.
The bell will sound. I will go to my doom.

O come my blond basket, o my rosy sky!
Visit your one condemned to death in this night.
Tear your flesh, kill, climb, fight,
But come! Against my round head pose your thigh.

We hadn't put our talk of love away,
We had gitanes but never lit them.
One wonders how the courts condemn
An assassin so fair that he pales the day.

Love come in my mouth! Love open your eaves,
Traverse the corridors, descend, light as a bird,

Fly down the staircase suppler than a shepherd,
Sustained better in the air than a flight of dead leaves.

O traverse the walls, if need be, walk the edges breadth
Of roofs, of oceans, cover yourself in light,
Use prayer, use menace to affright,
But come, o my frigate, an hour before my death.

The assassins of the wall envelop themselves in sun
In my cell, open to the chanting of high pines
That lulls, caught by the gilt lines
Knotted by the mariners that the clear morning's spun.

Who engraved a Rose of Winds into the gypsum wall?
Who dreams of my house in the depths of Hungary?
What child rolled upon my pallet of poverty?
And the instant of awakening old friends did recall?

Stray my Folly, for my joy creating
A consolate hell, peopled with gorgeous soldiers,
Naked to the belt and with the skivvies' odors
Reeking from those heavy flowers that strike me like lightning.

Wrestle out the worst mad acts from god knows who,
Kidnap some children, invent some torture,
Mutilate Beauty, torment her figure,
And give Guyana to the dudes for their rendezvous.

O sweet capital Cayenne! O my old Maroni River!
I see the hunched bodies of fifteen to twenty faggots
Surround a cute blond who smokes the butts
That the guards spit out into the moss and flowers.

A wet butt is sufficient to bring us all to gloom.
Alone, erect amongst the ferns tough and stiff,
The youngest is poised, leaning back on his slender hips,
Listless and waiting to become the sacred bridegroom.

And the old assassins rush forth with a brittle stick
To the evening's ceremony, squatting over a sordid
bit of live fire, stolen by their clever kid,
Purer and more arousing than an aroused prick.

With his polished muscles, the bandit most bold
Bows in respect before the frail boy. He is pleased.
The moon climbs in the sky. A quarrel is appeased.
The black flag waves in mysterious folds.

You envelop yourself so finely. Your gestures of lace!
A blushing palm tree one shoulder leans against.
You smoke. From your throat issues the fumes' ascent
While the convicts dance at a solemn pace.

Grave and mute, child, one after the other
They take from your mouth one drop, embalmed,
One drop, not two, of the vapor so profound
Floating off your tongue. O triumphant brother.

Terrible divinity, invisible and unpleasant,
You remain impassive, piercing, cast of clearest metal,
Attentive only to yourself, retailer of the fatal,
Transported on the filament of your hammock that rants.

Your delicate soul lies beyond the hills,
Still attending the spellbinding escape
Of one shot through the lungs after his jailbreak,
Lying dead, not thinking of you, in a valley's rills.

Elevate in the aura of the moon, O my changeling,
Roll over my love, come to my mouth to leak
A bit of heavy sperm from your throat to my teeth
To fecundate at long last our divine wedding.

Press your ravishing body against mine, mortifying,
From fucking the most tender and sweetest swindlers,
From beneath the weight of your balls, those round blond charmers,
Just up to your heart my black marble dick slides, impaling.

O take aim at sundown at the erect burnt out stud
And come to consume me! I've no time left for fools,
If you dare, come on, come out of your pools,
your swamps, where you make blisters of mud.

Souls of those I've slain! Kill me! Tend my cremation!
I've sculpted in life, like emaciated Michelangelo,

But as for Beauty, Lord, I've always served her so,
My guts, my knees, my hands, roses of emotion.

The cock's in the chicken coop, the Gallic pigeon,
The milkman's bottles, a bell in the air,
A footstep on the gravel, my window white and clear,
It's the joyous light shining on the slate-colored prison.

Gentlemen! I have no fear! If my head were rolling
In the ringing of the hamper along with your white face,
Mine fortunately would be resting on your haunch of grace,
Or for even more beauty, on your neck, my fowling.

Watch it! Tragic King, mouth half open,
I have access to your gardens of sand, so desolate,
Where you masturbate alone and two fingers elevate
Your head concealed in a veil of blue linen.

In an idiotic delirium, I see your exact double.
Love! Song! My Queen! Is this a male specter
Who examines me thus from the wall of plaster,
Glimpsed in your pale eyes as they started to ogle?

Don't become rigorous, let the matins be sung
In your bohemian heart, grant me just one kiss.
My God, I'm to croak without having had the bliss
Of holding you to heart and my crotch so well hung.

Forgive me, my God, for I have sinned.
The tears in my voice, my fever, my sufferance,
The wrong of my having to leave dear France,
Isn't this enough, Lord, to let me lie at journey's end?
            Weighted down with hope, perchance.

In your embalmed arms, in your chateaux of snow!
Lord of obscure reasons, still I know how to pray,
It is I, my Father, who exclaimed that one day,
Glory to highest heaven, for God who protects me below,
            Hermes, of the tender-footed way.

Of death I demand peace, the longest rest,
The chant of seraphim, their perfumes, their wreaths,

Woolen cherubim, in warm greatcoats, whom I hope bequeath
Only nights that are moonless and sunless
      Upon denatured heaths.

It isn't this morning I go to the guillotine.
I can sleep in, serenely. On the floor right above me
My idle minion, my pearl, Jesus who loves me
Wakes up. In his jackboots, hard and mean,
      He'll thrash my shorn skull, and kick and shove me.

It seems that an epileptic lives next-door to me.
The prison sleeps standing in a requiem's necromancing.
If sailors at sea can see ports advancing,
Towards another America my sleepers will flee.

Tennessee Williams

(1911 – 1985)

Considered Twentieth Century America's leading playwright, Thomas Lanier Williams began as a poet. His stories, novels and dramatic work are highly poetic, and he continued to write poetry all his life. His two poetry collections, In the Winter of Cities *(1964) and* Androgyne, Mon Amour *(1977) include lyric love poems and worldly, gently sardonic narratives. His* Memoirs, *published in 1975, scandalized some with their open homosexuality and erotic reminiscences.*

The Interior of the Pocket

It will not be necessary for you to look very far for the boy.
You will probably find him standing close to where you last saw him,
his attitude changed only slightly, his left hand removed
from the relatively austere pocket of the blue jacket
and thrust now into the more companionable pocket of the gray pants
so that the glazed material is drawn tight
over the rather surprisingly tenderly sculptured thigh...

The interior of the pocket is dark as the dark room he longs to
    sleep in;
it is dark as obliteration of something deeper than sense,
but in it the hot white hand of the boy is closed on itself
with a betrayal of tension his eyes have refused to betray,

for his eyes have not betrayed him. They are somewhat softer than blue
and they stay with the afternoon that fades about him, they take its
    color,
they even fade with its color as pieces of sky or water...
They show what nakedness is when a thing is truly naked,
and by the very completeness of its exposure is covered up,
when nothing being not seen makes nothing seen...

But while you watch him from your respectful distance,
as though he were an experiment in a glass, held over a flame,
about to change, to darken in color or cloud,

a motion occurs under the pocket's dark cover:
the hot white fingers unclose, they come unknotted and they extend
slightly sidewise, to offer again their gesture of reassurance
to that part of him, crestfallen, on which he depends
for the dark room he longs to sleep in,

the way small animals nudge one another at night,
as though to whisper, *We're close! There is still no danger!*

Androgyne, Mon Amour

I

Androgyne, mon amour,
brochette de coeur was plat du jour,
        (heart lifted on a metal skewer,
        encore saignante et palpitante)
where I dined au solitaire,
table intime, one rose vase,
        lighted dimly, wildly gay,
as, punctually, across the bay
mist advanced its pompe funèbre,
its coolly silvered drift of gray,
        nightly requiem performed for
mourners who have slipped away...

Well, that's it, the evening scene,
mon amour, Androgyne.

        Noontime youths,
thighs and groins tight-jean-displayed,
        loiter onto Union Square,
junkies flower-scattered there,
        lost in dream, torso-bare,
young as you, old as I, voicing soundlessly
a cry,
        oh, yes, among them
revolution bites its tongue beneath its fiery
        waiting stare,
indifferent to siren's wail,

ravishment endured in jail.
      Bicentennial salute?
Youth made flesh of crouching brute.

(Dichotomy can I deny of pity in a lustful eye?)

     II

Androgyne, mon amour,
shadows of you name a price
exorbitant for short lease.
What would you suggest I do,
wryly smile and turn away,
fox-teeth gnawing chest-bones through?

Even less would that be true
than, carnally, I was to you
many, many lives ago,
requiems of fallen snow.

And, frankly, well, they'd laugh at me,
thick of belly, thin of shank,
spectacle of long neglect,
tragedian to public mirth.

(Chekhov's *Mashas* all wore black
for a reason I suspect:
Pertinence? None at all—
yet something made me think of that.)

"Life!" the gob exclaimed to Crane,
"Oh, life's a geyser!"
     Oui, d'accord—
from the rectum of the earth.

Bitter, that. Never mind.
Time's only challenger is time.

III

Androgyne, mon amour,
cold withdrawal is no cure
for addiction grown so deep.
Now, finally, at cock's crow,
released in custody of sleep,
dark annealment, time-worn stones
      far descending,
no light there, no sound there,
entering depths of thinning breath,
farther down more ancient stones,
halting not, drawn on until

      Ever treacherous, ever fair,
      at a table small and square,
not first light but last light shows
(meaning of the single rose
where I dined au solitaire,
sous l'ombre d'une jeunesse perdue?)

      A ghostly little customs-clerk
      ("Vos documents, Mesdames, Messieurs?")
      whose somehow tender mockery
contrives to make admittance here
      at this mineral frontier
a definition of the pure...

      Androgyne, mon amour.

San Francisco, 1976

"Winter Smoke is Blue and Bitter"

Winter smoke is blue and bitter:
women comfort you in winter.

Scent of thyme is cool and tender:
girls are music to remember.

Men are made of rock and thunder:
threat of storm to labor under.

Cypress woods are demon-dark:
boys are fox-teeth in your heart.

James Broughton

(1913 –

James Broughton is sui generis *among gay poets. Through a long poetic and filmmaking career, he has developed into a bardic philosopher and something of a wizard figure. His unique style—prophetic, passionate and playful—is suggested by titles like* Graffiti for the Johns of Heaven *and* The Potted Psalm. *During the '80s and '90s he has become an important figure in the movement to explore a new gay spirituality which also nourishes the heart and embraces the flesh. He lives with his longtime lover and soul-mate, Joel Singer, in Port Townsend, Washington.*

Two Adams in a Sonoma Wood

Under the windsong of the redwood trees
we were two Adams together clinging
in the long nakedness of afternoon

Rediscovering close harmony
fingers practiced fresh arpeggios
nipples shone from riper torsos
loins opened into full bloom
Never had sweat tasted so juicy
or prolonged kiss so penetrant

Who in Eden lives for fashion
for investment   for notoriety?
Who is planning to go anywhere?

Reciprocal in savoring
we explored carnal phenomena
murmured unsayable secrets
tossed raptures back and forth
drank from each other's auras
till we purred with the hum of the world

Two seasoned lovers clinging together
renewed their Adamness on a bed of fern
under the windsong of the ancient trees

The Word for No Is Yes
Letter to a Young Poet Contemplating Suicide

I know a boy whose heart trembles, troubles and tricks him,
who leans over uncertain waters questioning his reflection,
whose long achings fill the night with ungraspable stars,
who tethers his faun at a sheltered bed of thistle and thorn,
unleashes that faun fitfully, fearful of what is not dream.
I know a boy whose heart startles, stirs and strangles him.

But there is a place where, believe me, heart and mind meet,
there is a place where the bloodstream and spirit embrace,
there is a place at the source of the lonely fountain
where the marriage of fire and water liberates the event.
In the realm of the fiercest oppositions, believe me,
the word for No is Yes, and the star and the faun are One.

Memento of an Amorist

When the young interviewer wanted to know
how he occupied his time in retirement
the ailing novelist sat up on his couch
to enjoy a guffaw before he spoke.

I haven't a retiring bone in my body.
I still slip out to pay my respects
to the beauties passing across the world.
Bless all mothers of shapely offspring.
I've never met a cock I didn't like.

Oh, said the reporter, may I quote that?

Say that I give compassionate attention
to mankind's need for a taste of bliss.
Don't you appreciate a friendly fondle?
To expect some love in return? Oh no.
I never look for a lover. I am one.

But sir, isn't such behavior risky?

Don't flinch, dear fellow. Learn to adore.
Adoration is life's healthiest behavior.
Wherever you go be a passionate lover
of whatever happens or whoever it is.
You'll grin all the way to your grave.

When he was later assigned the obituary
the journalist read in the suicide note:
I never learned to distinguish between
illusion and miracle. I didn't need to.
I trusted in love's confusing joy.

Coming in for a Landing

Though no pilot guarantees a bumpless arrival
or a key to the city at the terminal gate
I have journeyed this far with my carry-ons intact
by following my nose   trusting my flight plan
and holding my end up to face the music

My itineraries   my romances   my criminal records
were how I made a clearing in the wilderness of youth
to colonize a playground for my antic nature.
(If I weren't a jokester with a thoughtful mind
I would have no meaning and I wouldn't be me.)

At birth I swore allegiance to the visionary life
because it required neither logic nor geometry
so I live with ample rhyme but very little reason.
Though unscientific and financially unsound
I'm fitter than most old fiddles you can play with.

I live in Ambivalence   a mixed community
over the hills beyond the opposites
where all the streets run in both directions.
Loyal I am to the government of Imagination
and long in the service of Eros and Psyche.

In every bed that my life has tried lying in
the embrace of lust held the holiest of marvels
so that has been my faith since first I saw a phallus
rise out of a man and throb at the sky.
What else keeps the jewelry glowing in the lotus?

Without passionate hunger life's a munch on the run.
So the only baggage I claim is my aphrodisiac-pack
with its succulent tricks for uplifting the heart.
Do I go too far?   Do I want too much?
Too much has always been just enough for me.

Till the Captain brings me down and turns off my motor
I will cling to the banqueting wings of desire.

Litany for the Lord of My Chakras

Daily I chant a mantra to
  elevate his host
  inside my flesh
  from anus to cranium
Daily I stroke his lovepoints
  along my torso
  to stir ardent fire in
  the circuits of my soul

I arouse
  Jesus   in my perineum
  Hermes   in my penis
  Beloved   in my colon
  Bridegroom   in my stomach
  Androgyne   in my heart
  Poet   in my throat
  Redeemer   in my brow
  Godhead   in my crown

Every morning I summon
  his powers out of me
  and feel them rise to
  the touching of his names

With radiance he graces me
      loving himself in me
Radiantly I embrace him
      loving myself in him.

I call forth
  Jesus Hermes
    Beloved Bridegroom
      Androgyne Poet
        Redeemer Godhead
till rectum and nimbus connect
till the lotus shakes the root
till Above and Below ignite one another
  and my body leaps into
    steady flame
    ready to dance

Harold Norse

(1916 –

In his stupendous Memoirs of a Bastard Angel, Harold Norse describes how he picked up a shy 18-year-old Allen Ginsberg on the New York subway in 1944 and brought him to his room. In Provincetown that summer, Harold roomed with an unknown Tennessee Williams to whom he lent a buck for the trip back to New York to sell The Glass Menagerie. Norse's translations of the Italian GG Belli's poems influenced the Beats and even the academics when they appeared in the prestigious Hudson Review in 1956. A resident and collaborator with William Burroughs at the famous Beat Hotel, Harold is noted both for his "cut-up" novel, Beat Hotel, and his poems.
He resides in San Francisco.

To Mohammed at the Café Central

Tangier
sun and wind
strike the Medina mosque

Mohammed
seventeen years old
puffs his kif pipe
sipping green mint tea
where blue phallic arches
rise among white walls
and berber rugs

the muezzin traces ALLAH
thru the moon's
loudspeaker
over casbah roofs
of Socco Chico

moneylenders
sip mint tea

but Mohammed's eye
brilliant and black
darts among tourists
for a simpático friend
and glances at transistors
covetously
and tattooed mammas
you-youing
papoosed in laundrybags
peeping thru djellabas

the crescent sun
on lightning terraces
dries everything
in a second!

Tangier/Paris, 1962

To Mohammed on Our Journeys

I was the tourist
el simpático
and your brother offered you
and also himself
I forgot about your brother
and we took a flat in the Marshan
with reed mats and one water tap
about a foot from the floor
and we smoked hasheesh
and ate well and loved well
and left for the south
Essaouira, Fez, Marrakech
and got to Taroudant
thru the mountains
and bought alabaster kif bowls
for a few dirhams and watched
the dancing boys in desert cafés
kissing old Arabs and sitting on their
laps, dancing with kohl eyes
and heard the music down in Jejouka

in the hills under the stars
the ancient ceremony, Pan pipes
fierce in white moonlight
by white walls
with hooded figures
stoned on kif
for eight nights
and the goatboy in a floppy hat
scared us, beating the air
with a stick, beating whoever came close,
Father of Skins, goat god,
and the flutes maddened us
and we slept together in huts

San Francisco, 7.xi.72

To Mohammed in the Hotel of the Palms

behind the glass wall
                                    i see blue limbs
                                    black fungus noses
            thighs knee caps
                        "i have the taste of the infinite"
ylem
            primordial squinch   the universe crushed into
                                                            a seed
nothing will satisfy me
                        i write green ballets & hollow journeys
caught in the etheric web of yr crotch
                        a hairy ocean of darkness

                                    doors of pearl
                        open to fiery radiance
majoun madness
            down marrakech alleys
      the   djemaa el fna
squirming   with snakes
          in carbide glow

black gnaoua dancers!   lash sword!   flash teeth!

under the barrow
    broiling in sleep   mouth
& nostrils buzzing with flies
                    genitals thick swollen
out of big tear in pants
            derelict 14 yr old street arab
    cameras snapping
   like teeth

  who are you
        little arab
        i shared my visions
                and ate
      black hasheesh candy with
the doors of yr body   flung open
      we twitched in spasms
        muscular convulsions
          heavenly epilepsy on the bed
   in the hotel of the palms
     prolonged orgasm
      uncontrollable joy
           of leaving the mind

Athens, 1965

To Mohammed at the Height

the moment widens—your voice
VAST across the room—my
head explodes into con
scious speed an ache
shoots along the
nerve of my left eye pushing to
the center above my nose—
your browngold skin
dance flute laugh
    yes
everything lives
because I love you

ALL
levels
at once
brain flickers
nosebridge pinches
bright cells full of happening
this can not
END

Tangier/Paris, 1962

To Mohammed at Parting

the wind hurls through the straits
white ruffs on greenblue
water I will cross
to Spain

your bag is packed for the bus
to Melilla
back to the Rif

I see your mountain hut
the scrawny sheep
rugged Berber tribesmen
scrape in the fields
you will scrape

bye bye Mouniria
so long kid

Tangier/Paris, 1962

Byron Alfonso

The dance you did in the mirror
the ancient Mayas might have done
        or the decadent Atlanteans
before the continent slipped
                        into the sea
the pagan dance
                that bypassed time
        (ancient disco fever)

A god entered you
                as you entered me

old satyr and young faun
        sharing the mysteries
                bypassing laws

drunken-stoned temple dancer
young male whore
        reviving the ritual
                with cannabis

rubbing your smooth body
against my furry one

smell of goats and satyrs

                gleaming sweat

with each step
                and bent thigh
the god rises
                and resurrects

the grunting dance
                of erections

Guatemala City, 1979

You Must Have Been a Sensational Baby

1
I love your eyebrows, said one.
the distribution of your body hair
is sensational. what teeth, said two.
your mouth is cocaine, said three.
your lips, said four, look like sexual organs.
they are, I said.
as I got older features thickened.
the body grew flabby. then
thin in the wrong places. they
all shut up or spoke about life.

2
a pair of muscular calves
drove me crazy today.
I studied their size, their shape,
their suntanned hairiness. I spoke
to the owner of them. are you
a dancer? I asked. oh no,
I was born with them, he said.
you must have been a sensational baby,
I said. he went back to his newspaper.
I went back to his calves.
he displayed them mercilessly.
he was absolutely heartless.
men stole secret looks at them.
women pretended he was a table.
they all had a pained expression.
he went on reading the Sports Page.
his thighs were even more cruel
thrust brutally from denim shorts.
the whole place trembled with lust.

San Francisco, 1973

Big Thick Dick

Big Thick Dick & Tasty Jr. Bear
Hairy & Sweet Delectable Indeed
And Dirty Mouth Showoff Awesome Gypsie Top
Big Irish Hung Like You'd Hope & Black Body Builder
For Muscle Worship Super Safe Mega Dick
And Creamy French Delicacy Horse Hung For Dessert
Plus Uncut & Hungry Fantasies Fulfilled
You'll Go WOOF! For This Smooth Blond Nice & Nasty Stud
And Rock Hard Professional Cleancut Gym Studs Waiting For You
A Man For All Reasons Bigger Is Better Indulge Yourself
All Scenes Considered Eat at Pete's Low Hangers
Or Bubble Butt Boy Toy Handsome Student Body
Or Prime Hot Rod Therapeutic & Erotic
Or Asian Dream Hairy Russian Rodeo Cowboy
French Marine German Master Rican Masseur
Eros + Agape Double Pleasure Body Magic
Affirm Self Love Sing The Body Mechanic & Surrender
Unravel With Stressbuster Deep Throat Man To Man
Warm Hands Warm Heart Warm Head Warm Butt Warm Rod
Nurturing Touch In Finest Tradition of Bodywork
Ahhh...Slow.Sensual.Complete.Ecstatic.Hot.Close.
Nips Aching For Touch? Call Bearcub or Dick of Death
Or Nebraska Farm Boy or Ragin' Cajun or Dungeon Dragon
Big Holiday Sale More For LE$$ You'll Feel Real Good

San Francisco, 1996

*[This is a "cut-up" poem, i.e. the words and phrases were cut out at random
from a gay newspaper, ads and personals, and put together as an invented
"poem." HN]*

Robert Duncan

(1919 – 1988)

Robert Duncan was one of the first out-of-the-closet American writers. He created controversy as early as 1944 with his essay "The Homosexual in Society," published in Dwight Macdonald's magazine Politics. *Duncan later became a leading figure in the "San Francisco Renaissance" and taught at the influential Black Mountain College. His intellectual, often elliptical, poetry is pervaded by hermetic philosophy and by Duncan's love for his longtime partner, the painter Jess Collins.*

Sonnet 1

Now there is a Love of which Dante does not speak unkindly,
Tho it grieves his heart to think upon men
      who lust after men and run
      —his beloved Master, Brunetto Latini, among them—
Where the roaring waters of hell's rivers
Come, heard as if muted in the distance,
      like the hum of bees in the hot sun.

Scorcht in whose rays and peeld, these would-be lovers
Turn their faces, peering in the fire-fall,
      to look to one another
As men searching for an other
      in the light of a new moon look.

Sharpening their vision, Dante says, like a man
      seeking to thread a needle,
They try the eyes of other men
Towards that eye of the needle
      Love has appointed there
For a joining that is not easy.

The Torso   Passages 18

Most beautiful!   the red-flowering eucalyptus,
          the madrone, the yew

      Is he...

So thou wouldst smile, and take me in thine arms
The sight of London to my exiled eyes
Is as Elysium to a new-come soul

                If he be Truth
                I would dwell in the illusion of him

His hands unlocking from chambers of my male body

          such an idea in man's image

      rising tides that sweep me towards him

                ...*homosexual?*

                      and at the treasure of his mouth

          pour forth my soul

                      his soul   commingling

I thought a being more than vast, His body leading
          into Paradise,   his eyes
                quickening a fire in me,   a trembling

      hieroglyph: At the root of the neck

      the clavicle, for the neck is the stem of the great artery
          upward into his head that is beautiful

                At the rise of the pectoral muscles

      the nipples, for the breasts are like sleeping fountains
          of feeling in man, waiting above the beat of his heart,
          shielding the rise and fall of his breath, to be
          awakend

At the axis of his mid hriff

the navel, for in the pit of his stomach the chord from
which first he was fed has its temple

At the root of the groin

the pubic hair, for the torso is the stem in which the man
flowers forth and leads to the stamen of flesh in which
his seed rises

a wave of need and desire over   taking me

cried out my name

(This was long ago.   It was another life)

and said,

What do you want of me?

I do not know, I said.   I have fallen in love.   He
has brought me into heights and depths my heart
would fear   without him.   His look

pierces my side   •   fire eyes   •

I have been waiting for you, he said:
I know what you desire

you do not yet know   but through me   •

And I am with you everywhere.   In your falling

I have fallen from a high place.   I have raised myself

from darkness in your   rising

wherever you are

my hand in your hand   seeking   the locks, the keys

I am there.   Gathering me, you gather

your Self   •

For my Other is not a woman but a man

the King upon whose bosom let me lie.

This Place Rumord to have Been Sodom

   might have been.
Certainly these ashes might have been pleasures.
Pilgrims on their way to the Holy Places remark
this place. Isn't it plain to all
that these mounds were palaces? This was once
a city among men, a gathering together of spirit.
It was measured by the Lord and found wanting.

It was measured by the Lord and found wanting,
destroyd by the angels that inhabit longing.
Surely this is Great Sodom where such cries
as if men were birds flying up from the swamp
ring in our ears, where such fears that were once
desires walk, almost spectacular,
stalking the desolate circles, red eyed.

This place rumord to have been a City surely was,
separated from us by the hand of the Lord.
The devout have laid out gardens in the desert,
drawn water from springs where the light was blighted.
How tenderly they must attend these friendships
or all is lost. All *is* lost.
Only the faithful hold this place green.

Only the faithful hold this place green
where the crown of fiery thorns descends.
Men that once lusted grow listless. A spirit
wrappd in a cloud, ashes more than ashes,
fire more than fire, ascends.

Only these new friends gather joyous here,
where the world like Great Sodom lies under fear.

The world like Great Sodom lies under Love
and knows not the hand of the Lord that moves.
This the friends teach where such cries
as if men were birds fly up from the crowds
gatherd and howling in the heat of the sun.
In the Lord Whom the friends have named at last Love
the images and loves of the friends never die.

This place rumord to have been Sodom is blessd
in the Lord's eyes.

James Kirkup

(1919 –

A prolific, cosmopolitan writer, James Kirkup has spent much of his life in the Far East, publishing travel books and memoirs of several Asian countries, as well as poems, novels, plays, children's books, anthologies and autobiography. His early romantic verse was succeeded by explicitly gay and political poems, one of which,
"The Love That Dares to Speak Its Name," *led to the 1977 prosecution of* Gay News *under the English blasphemy laws. He currently resides in Andorra.*

Camping Out

Never having had anything in common with
life here below, I used to wear
stiletto heels with my Mackintosh tartan kilt,
black lipstick on my upper lip,
white on the bottom
(lip, I mean)—
violet fishnet elbow-length evening gloves
with colossal junk jewelry rings
worn conveniently on the outside.

Shaved my lissom legs right up to the navel
rimmed with opalescent rainbow paillettes
then painted a straight black seam
all down their slinky length.
My demure *poitrine*, my seductive *derriere*
powdered with minisculest sequins,
the three nipples rouged in contrasting tones
of stop—caution—go.

On my proud head with its flawless face
made up like a Picasso lady's
(when I don't have blue I use green)
what is both wig and picture hat, perfumed and
thermostatically controlled to suit the seasons.
And over all, flung with a gay abandon,

my mile-long scintillating feathered boa
imitating—nay, rivaling—the entire
sky at night, with numerous Milky Ways.

Thus clothed and almost in my right mind,
each inch-long fingernail a different hue,
I used to prepare each day to face
this ball-breaking existence some called life
mistakenly foisted upon us by some Almighty sod
in which—a virgin orphaned at the age of fifty—
with no fixed abode, no regular employment
and no apparent means of subsistence
I have always considered myself
to be nothing more than
patiently, elegantly, contemptuously
camping out.

Gay Boys

Those two young men, dancing quietly together in a corner
To the slow fox of *'Moonlight on the Ruined Castle'*
Are nice to watch—I don't know why—in this gay but ghastly bar.
Something in their close embrace's calm
Neutrality is more than moving: a perfect unconcern, their bodies'
Innocent conspiracy, appears to make them twins,
Their pale monkey faces mischievous and pure
Beneath the hair's black tomboy fringe.

Image of an ideal that is not only Greek,
They preserve an oriental poise, involuntary ignorance
Of private misery. Behind the sooty fans of their tilted lids'
Peculiar inclinations, their eyes dark ellipses slightly
Shift, like leaves glimpsed through holes in a paper screen.
Their pale mouths curve, flowers of blotted ink,
Into each other's cheeks. At the tips of their fine hands
The brown fingers make their nails bright pink.

Neither guilt nor passion moves them, neither do they think
Of happiness, a concept unnecessary to enjoyment.

Untroubled creatures of the spirit's jungle,
They neither smile nor weep, but turn their open masks
To look no further than the moment and each other,
Mirroring the long, cool record's easy play.
Knowing no reason why they should not be so,
They dance together, and are truly gay.

Elegy for Pier Paolo Pasolini
(murdered, Rome, November 2, 1975)

So Momma Roma got you in the end—
the bitch goddess and her instrument,
a bit of teenage rough trade, one of those
subproletarian *ragazzi da vita* you immortalized
in poetry and film—one of your own sorry passions.

Sex for you, as for so many of us,
was pure pleasure, uncontaminated by
the bourgeois shams of guilt, family and home;
but also a religious and political commitment—
each one-night stand a separate responsibility for life, and man.

I know too well the station where you picked him up, (or he
picked you), that fascinating messenger from ancient furies.
The gay guides are filled with places just the same,
where lust and destiny, danger and boredom all
come together in a final massacre of loneliness.

Una vita violenta—your own title
for the sad brutality of fallen Rome
that is forever ancient, ruined by the scandal of perverse
papal prohibitions, by the moon's castrating goddess
who allowed a first and final grope, then excommunicated you—

crushed you to death in the suburban cruelty and moonless dark
of Ostia, pathetic substitute and shabby back-projection for
what should have been mysterious and scented pagan groves,
with high priests chanting, dancing, performing a rotten rite
on naked Adonises, chained and ravished on altars of marble flowers.

—Instead, courageous and confessed comrade of boys and men,
compassionate Marxist-Sodomist of all male Christian love,
you in a pious odour of sanctity were hypocritically laid to rest
in Rome, according to the last rites of a church that you so often
both loved and lashed, celebrated and despised.

—Yes, they fucked up the final cut, and the unkindest.
But in the memories of men, you, Pier Paolo,
the close-up victim of your own compulsions, hero
of your own divine poetic fantasies, forever cruise
infatuation's crowded boulevard of shadows

in your excessive chariot of love and death,
the moon-silvery Alfa Romeo, vehicle and property
of which your lonely genius and vision were the only stars,
and that you slowly faded out, in Ostia,
one Sunday night, in Scorpio, in winter, when the moon was dark.

Damn the Culture Ministry

My lover from Asakusa, a blooming boy,
He who adorned his amber body
With a swirling tattoo
Of the goddess Kwannon surrounded
By ferns, wildflowers, flags,
And had a capering carp
Illuminating each vigorous buttock—

He whose suit of ink,
Blue and black and dogrose pink,
Was the one garment
I could not divest him of—
When he pulled back
His periwinkled foreskin, he discovered,
Always with a broken smile,
A gay butterfly on the *glans penis*.

Now the Cultural Ministry
Has proclaimed him
Not only a National Treasure, but
An Intangible National Treasure!

Now I can no longer
Hold him in my arms like a warm
Sheaf of poppies and wheat, no more
Stroke that golden-amber shoulder
Stained with a lace of sugarbag blue,
No more bedew
With tears and kisses his
Empurpled butterfly...

I can't get my hands on him.
Our love is finished,
Broken by banal politicians.

Now he belongs to the Nation,
Which means he belongs to no one,
And especially not to me.
I always put him on a pedestal,
But not like this!
He might as well be behind glass,
Stuffed and docketed in the National Museum.

Damn the Culture Ministry!

Kirby Congdon

(1924 –

Published by gay magazines and small presses, Kirby Congdon's work has always existed on the margins. Much of his writing expresses a fascination with the character and personalities of animals and machines. The prophetic prose poems of Dream-Work *(1970) and* Fantoccini *(1980), capturing a sadomasochistic delirium whose central image is the motorcycle, have become underground classics. Congdon is also a sculptor and a bibliographer of motorcycle books.*

Motorcyclist

The intoxicating stench of gas
mixes with the body's sweat
and smell of musk.
Their leather torsos,
riding iron bulls,
intimate and crouched,
intense in the lover's act,
copulate with their hot machines.
Blood and oil are one.
They eat and digest
death.

Motorcyclists

burn tire tracks
through my guts;
roar, exhausting,
under rearing buttocks;
cut corners
across my taut chest;
like roving lovers,

leave me, strapped,
silent and stranded.
Their intricate engines
are merciless,
blasting through
the insides of my torn-out heart,
ripping ragged holes
out of the night,
shaking space
with black sound
across the asphalt of heaven,
their staccatos scattering
sparks, hearts, stars.

Daredevil

Hard helmets and high boots
tumescent in the sun,
got-up in rubber skin
and leather hide,
black, strapped, laced,
buckled with grommets,
chrome and brassy-eyed,
their dress itself is an act of sex,
as the body, used,
tumbles to its end
like jointed dolls we outgrew
and threw aside.
So the exalted race
to their base death
in self-abuse begins,
as the body's transient existence
sings its violent end,
to replace that dull, dull death
that waits upon the rest of us
behind a desk,
behind another desk,
behind the coffin's lid
closing like an office door.

The Motorcycle Social Club

After the run, we all meet at the Club—those of us who haven't broken down, dropped their bikes, or gotten hurt, injured or killed. We play pool and drink, and move in even strides about the room, showing off the thick backs of our curving thighs, gleaming where the black leather stretches tight. We spend the evening sending messages—flowers, emergency telegrams and time-bombs—with our eyes. When we pair off, we are casual and conceal the excitement we feel at our public but silent commitment to destruction. The veteran members disappear one by one to recover in hometowns, or to wait in hospitals or graves. But the membership grows, though the initiations become more stringent. The local people laugh nervously at our public image, or they ask, Where will it all end? But the game, underneath, is serious and there is no end. In the land of plenty, death grows, fertilized and lush. And we get drunk on the habit-forming perfumes of its secret and majestic, its black and addictive blooms, and each flower broken off sheds a glittering shower of hard new seeds. There's the fascination. To join the Club is difficult; to be a member is final and permanent. Meanwhile, as we wait for our own last night, we drink and play pool.

Jagannath

...and when, after years of developing it, he had molded every contour of his body to perfection, marveling in the cold mirror the taut curves of the pectorals, the lean, hard undulations of his abdomen, and the restrained power of his swollen thighs, with hypnotic fascination— almost greed—in his eyes, he pushed his middle finger under his testicles, into his rectum and pressed forward. So, he ejaculated before the mirror, and as often as possible. His eyes gobbled up all the different and perfected sections of his straining body until, throwing his head back, and rising on his toes, his pelvis shoved forward, the semen jerked out like his very soul, arching in space, thick in its glorious waste, uniting itself with the empty air like far-flung and briefly luminous constellations which fell in their destruction with soft splats against the mirror and onto the floor until he doubled over in exhaustion and then leaned, breathing heavily, against the wall and watched his body slowly relax its magnificent tensions.

He exercised and manipulated his beauty every day, sharing it only in the sidelong glance of strangers who watched his athletic movements or caught a glimpse of his body which revealed itself as a living explication of the human form—to be handled and coddled and toyed with, roughed about and teased and mistreated until that body broke in its purest function and lay, still beautiful, like a great imaginary landscape, with a thigh or a breastplate glistening with his own body's juice where, far-flung, it had landed and was just beginning to leak out from its own heavy substance, to define a muscle's shape like a painful tear. Obsessed with himself, he was happy to enjoy the workings of his interior body, to have those strange unknown motors move, run, churn and race, pumping up a wellful of compressed sludge until this volcano of lava vomited up his very loins under the studied, shameless gaze of his one admirer in the mirror.

But now he found a silent place in a desert area, on a hill-top close to heaven which looked down on him with its great indifferent eyes, pretending not to care or to watch, as he removed his clothes. Lying down, he inserted the gun barrel into his rectum and aggravated himself in an almost ugly and mean fashion, his fist on his erect cock, stroking and twisting it cruelly over and over again to the breaking point, releasing his hand just quickly enough to forestall an ejaculation, as the head of the penis alternately shone with its anticipatory lubricant.

Finally, as the afternoon wore on, he knew it was time. He rested until all was quiet and relaxed so that he could appreciate the full sweep of his excitement. He began slowly and forced himself not to rush his progress, and then he attacked his cock roughly, occasionally rolling over, the gravel scrubbing his driving-rod knuckles raw and the gun barrel jabbing his rectum compulsively. His throat clutched at the air in gasps as he felt his loins convulse at the center of his being. The throbs sped through his fingers where the semen rushed through his flaming cock in hard pellets. As the first glob seemed to push his thighs apart with its force, his cock broke out of his blinded hand and as the second burst fell on his body like fireworks, he pulled the trigger of the gun. Its one expensive bullet lunged its way deep into his stomach without time, and blasted a white hole that seemed larger than his own torso for the length of his prostrate body. His penis continued to break forth in ruptured joy until at last it subsided, and he was left for the rest of the afternoon bathed in his own sweat, under his own semen, and on top of his own blood, under the impassive sky which looked down on him as indifferently as before.

His pain lifted him out of himself, his brain a mass of shapeless fire, a molten, boiling stone of hideous sensitivity and feeling that swarmed over him and advanced and retreated like the sun moving in and out of focus, or like galaxies of time itself exploding and shrinking in the slow motions of astronomical speeds. In time, before the sun itself had set, he died.

When his admirer came from out of his mirror and found the corpse, he saw the position of the gun and understood. He looked close and saw where the semen had dried in shallow, almost invisible scabs on his still body. The visitor knelt down on the ground beside the body, withdrew his cock, waited dispassionately for it to grow full and large, and then covered the suicide once more with medallions of come. Then he removed his own clothes and lay down naked with the corpse for a while, chest to chest. Having regained his strength, he put his clothes back on and headed down the hill toward the town and the people.

It was a beautiful day, filled with love. It was holy and the people in it seemed, all of them, to be saints. And the dying and the dead—martyrs whom he alone had blessed and whose transfiguration he alone had witnessed, and whose meaninglessness he alone knew—had more meaning than existence itself—an existence which was the fulfillment of life into the very extremes of its far-flung boundaries, which are those far-off yet so close frontiers of death.

Horse-Opera

His very victims
also overcome,
drunk with death,
prostrate,
and past ecstasy,
the cowboy-hero, cool,
blows smoke
from his hot gun's barrel
that banged his leather-vested
partner/villain
down to dust,
and tucks the rod away

like a still-stiff cock
that's just shot off
its stinging load
into the second-man's entrails
and marries,
in love's hate,
and war's own peace,
his mirror's mate;
re-enacts a myth,
a play of words,
a game of wish
and all of it
hides love's hard kiss.

Autopyrotechnics

As I sat cross-legged before the universe,
reeking of gasoline, soaked in the gorgeous fashion
of the times, my public cock, demanding and merciless,
reached proudly to my navel.

I hardly had a chance to see the match ignite
before heaven and earth were enflowered in my own
body's extravagant flame.

Hero Comic

I am the hero,
death's antagonist.
My strength indestructible,
my body can not be broken.
My bones are iron.
All wounds are flesh
while my body's pornography
survives the current body's death.
I will not age or falter.
Adversity identifies my event.
I, hero, exist
in the art of my own myth,
in film, printed page, or comic strip
and, in miniature, in men,
when I bring them back
to their true lives again.

Edward Field

(1924 –

*A meditative, autobiographical poet, Edward Field has strongly influenced the
course of contemporary poetry with his eloquent classics of humorous eroticism
such as "The Moving Man" and "Giant Pacific Octopus," and his witty,
subversive pastiches of pop culture like "Nancy" and "Sweet Gwendolyn and
the Countess." His other work ranges from ruminations on Jewish themes to
translations of Eskimo folk stories.*

Street Instructions: At the Crotch

It is not against the law to grope yourself. — DDT

Remember yourself. — Gurdjieff

While walking toward housewife wielding baby
reach down and squeeze your cock,
looking at her casually.

Adjust cock from left side to right
causing half hard-on,
then shift it back.

Wear balls on one side, cock on other.

Tug at crotch of pants as if to free genitals
tangled in underwear.
Give it a good tugging.
Go out without underwear.

Make small tear in bulge of basket
exposing skin.
Sew patch on crudely.

Wear pants of some material
flimsy as the law allows.

Go out with fly unzippered.
Go out with fly half unbuttoned.
Break zipper and fasten with safety pins.
Rip crotch and sew with large jagged stitches.

While talking with friends
unzip fly, lower pants, and arrange shirt tails.

Ask policemen for directions
and while he's telling you
give yourself a feel.

Walk loosely
to give yourself as much stimulation as you can.
Let it all move.
Be there.

The Moving Man

He was a burly, curly-blond ape of a man
who had a moving van
and a bunch of young helpers he paid by the job.
He treated those boys like a harem,
picking one for his pleasure when he wanted.
He had wrestled them all to defeat
for when they fell under his weight
with that huge body on them
they went dreamy as desire took them,
and they let it.

Having him for example, they were a rowdy gang
hanging around the office at the front of the garage
waiting for a job to be called in,
always wrestling and grabbing at each other
with an eye cocked for the boss' approval,
half-teasing him with their slim bodies
muscled from the work.

The van stood behind in the shadows
with its tailgate down, empty
except for the quilts used to wrap furniture in,
lying in a heap.

In the idleness of the afternoon
the boss would start horsing around with a boy,
perhaps one who had been especially fresh,
and chasing him through the dark garage
force him right up the tailgate into the van.
There they fell rolling on the quilts
until the man, pinning him with his chest,
pulled down the boy's pants—
his own were always open.
His large hand roved down the naked belly
to the clutch of hair and hard-standing prick—
with balls, a handful—
and the boy yelped, but had to stay.

His wrestler arms tamed that young body like an animal:
Holding him prisoner, he forced him over,
his cock probing the backs of his thighs,
the cheeks of his ass,
thrusting all over to find the moist center.
One hand on a breast fingered the nipple,
the other arm pulled him closer below
to the hot push, demanding entrance.
His mouth bit at the boy's neck,
breathing hard on the plum of a cheek,
his stubble scratching as he growled in the boy's ear,
teaching him pleasure.

Now he held in his arms the whole boy
his fat prick pushed between those round cheeks,
until the boy, completely submerged in that loving hulk of a man,
relaxed with a moan and opened
and the moving man moved his prick all the way in,
taking his time.

Breakfast

I am sitting here at my desk in the morning as usual
with the tie-rack on the wall in front of me.
(L., which stands for love, is in the other room
writing his novel near the plants.)
My favorite green tie
that always makes my eyes luminous when I wear it
had its tail cut off by L.
because he said it grew too long.
His shoes always loosen, and his pants stretch;
he changes the size of everything, like he did my life.
He makes all things grow, I will testify to that.

I am good with plants however:
Where I love it is green.
Where L. loves
it grows like nebulae, expanding:
He gets bigger and bigger in my arms
like a Picasso nude that smacks you in the face with a tit
while the goodies of her body are breaking out all over,
her legs writhing in ecstasy: she is titled BREAKFAST.
And you look at all this,
it is absolute Heaven and you have it in your arms;
so you start kissing like mad just to hold it down,
and you find to your surprise that you didn't take off into space
but sank deliciously into a sea of luminous green,
into a garden you never grew, a garden that God gave you—
and you've got such a hard-on for this delightful youth
like you never knew was possible.

Old Acquaintance

> "Deirdre! Come out!
> Come out from behind that screen.
> I've been hiding behind screens
> since before you were born."
> —Bette Davis, in *"Old Acquaintance"*

Old friend, we've come through
in pretty good shape, so far,
better, in fact,
than during those angst-filled years
when you wrecked my life
and I wrecked yours. Remember?
But, back then, we didn't appreciate each other,
did we—like an ill-matched couple,
a bad job by an incompetent marriage broker,
or who just got married out of general horniness
rather than any real compatibility.

I never liked your looks or size
and you had ideas of your own
I couldn't figure out,
though I responded to your goading
and roamed the nights away.
My God, what you led me into,
and I got you into some pretty tight fixes myself.

Life is less strenuous now.
In our golden years, you make few demands.
We've both come to like a bit of a wank,
with none of the old recriminations after.
And I've even learned to admire,
as I pose in the mirror,
your silky length,
respect your sulky independence.
I wonder that I ever thought you
insufficient, myself underendowed—
or else you've grown.

Best of all, I'm impressed
by how good we look together—
the proportions seem just right.

So, Good Cock,
dick, prick, dong,
lul, bite, schwantz,
wang, willie, weenie,
and all your other names,
if you've a mind to, now,
and I'd say you've earned it,
stand up, old friend, with me
and take a bow.

Dirty Old Man

1

When I go senile, I swear I'm going to let go
and grope everything in sight—
the Italian waiter in his black trousers,
that soulful-eyed Hasid at the discount store,
the doctor leaning close to take my blood—
what I've had to hold back on all my life.

So what if they put me away
in a nursing home?
I'll feel up the attendants,
who well may think, Why not let him?
Don't do me no harm.

2

For once in my life
I'm going to be free
and grope everything in sight:
Let them cut off my hands,
palms still hairy from adolescent onanistic bouts,
I'll grope with my toes—
they'll have to amputate them one by one.
Then my tongue, my lips, my toothless gums.

Let them take away part after part,
something forbidden is still possible
with kneecaps, elbows, ears—
every part of me has a dirty mind.

And through it all I'll stare my fill
right up to when they seal my eyes.
They can cut out my heart, of course,
but even that's no guarantee:
My newly-liberated senile ghost
will go a-roving day and night.
And then what's to stop me groping
every man in sight?

Robert Peters

(1924 –

Robert Peters lives in southern California with his long-term life-mate, Scrabble pro and poet Paul Trachtenberg, where he continues to spin off memoirs for the University of Wisconsin Press. A now-retired English professor, famous for his in-costume poetry events, his poetry collections are too numerous to recount—he has no idea—as he currently works with Paul T on a companion dictionary volume for the first Alphabet Soup: A Laconic Lexicon for all Word Lovers.

Tommy McQuaker

Tommy McQuaker's soft fat dad
clerked at the bank.
His bosomy mother Pearl prattled.
Her orange hair was tightly curled.

In summer, Tommy
swished down Main Street
with a poodle on a leash.
He wore shorts, sandals,
and a polkadot tie.

We said he lacked balls
that he cupped his hands when he peed.
He was into theater and verse.
He had a "boyfriend" in Chicago.
That town's exotic.

I kept my distance from him,
as I did from Catholic nuns,
on the far side of the street.

I feared Tommy would bite my lips
and bestow awesome diseases.
I craved his obscene squeezes.

Carnival Man

I tried to lock the door.
The sound of whipped leaves was hard to bear.
I pounded my feet on the floor.
I should not have gone to the fair.

I had helped him erect the tent.
We both held the central pole.
He was Southern, brown, magnificent.
I was his branch, he was my bole.

I watched him undress in his trailer.
He thought I was older then.
He gave me two dollars for my labor,
and said "keep growing"—he'd be back again.

I couldn't lock the door.
Horses were loose in the storm.
I huddled on the floor.
I shouldn't have gone to the fair!

Night Visitor

Night sweat, hard breathing.
Agate moonlight shed through the window,
as the outlaw, white-throated,
in a white shirt with rolled sleeves
strokes the sleeping boy's shoulder.

He lifts the boy and holds him
sheetless, nude.
The boy tastes Dillinger's mouth,
the fleshed inner lip, the tongue,
the zinc-taste of saliva.
"Take me!" the boy pleads.
The creaking is the roof's wind,
the bronze spittle of home.

Cousins

They slept three to a bed.
Winter and summer they wore
split-seat union suits.
They were in their teens.
I was ten.

A late-spring storm. Severe.
My aunt says to stay over:
"You can sleep with my boys
in the big bed."

I undress in the dark, fear they'll mock
my pubic hairs, my tiny cock.
They doff their clothes, ready to sleep.
Albert is on the outside, Frenchy
in the middle, then Jim.
"Jump in."

I lie on my back.
Aromatic breaths.
I turn. Frenchy's rear is bare.
Albert snuggles. My heel touches
his balls. I pretend to sleep.
His penis hardens, snaking
my buttocks. My craving
funnels itself: sweat roils.
the sweet stench of ivory and leek.

Snapshot of Older Cousin Masturbating

He stands nude
on a tamarack log
poised over Minnow Lake
set to plunge.
He doesn't see me.
His throat is summer tan
as are his hands and chest.
His body ripples.

He's making hand motions,
jerking off. I ache to stroke him
and want his timing right.

We jerk with the same thrust:
globs of cream float away on the stream.
This is neither fantasy nor dream.

Nude Father

I've never stopped, even in my sleep,
seeing him in the lake
facing me with his hands all wax
over his sex. His throat and wrists
are sun burned. He is so white.
He splashes me with water.

I yank my baggy swim trunks off,
dive, and reach cold mud.
I hold a submerged tree branch.

I surface as he retrieves his clothes.
He keeps on walking, nude,
entices me to follow, at the rear.

Frank O'Hara

(1926 – 1966)

Frank O'Hara's position as a poet is interwoven with his profession as a curator and art critic. His witty, conversational poems reflect his intense involvement with popular culture, urban gay life and the New York art world. An influential poet, he died young (at 40, as he had predicted) after being hit by a dune buggy on Fire Island.

Having a Coke with You

is even more fun than going to San Sebastian, Irún, Hendaye, Biarritz,
     Bayonne
or being sick to my stomach on the Travesera de Gracia in Barcelona
partly because in your orange shirt you look like a better happier St.
     Sebastian
partly because of my love for you, partly because of your love for
     yoghurt
partly because of the fluorescent orange tulips around the birches
partly because of the secrecy our smiles take on before people and
     statuary
it is hard to believe when I'm with you that there can be anything as
     still
as solemn as unpleasantly definitive as statuary when right in front of it
in the warm New York 4 o'clock light we are drifting back and forth
between each other like a tree breathing through its spectacles

and the portrait show seems to have no faces in it at all, just paint
you suddenly wonder why in the world anyone ever did them
                                             I look
at you and I would rather look at you than all the portraits in the world
except possibly for the *Polish Rider* occasionally and anyway it's in the
     Frick
which thank heavens you haven't gone to yet so we can go together the
     first time
and the fact that you move so beautifully more or less takes care of
     Futurism

just as at home I never think of the *Nude Descending a Staircase* or
at a rehearsal a single drawing of Leonardo or Michelangelo that used
      to wow me
and what good does all the research of the Impressionists do them
when they never got the right person to stand near the tree when the
      sun sank
or for that matter Marino Marini when he didn't pick the rider as
      carefully
as the horse
        it seems they were all cheated of some marvellous experience
which is not going to go wasted on me which is why I'm telling you
      about it

Homosexuality

So we are taking off our masks, are we, and keeping
our mouths shut? as if we'd been pierced by a glance!

The song of an old cow is not more full of judgment
than the vapors which escape one's soul when one is sick;

so I pull the shadows around me like a puff
and crinkle my eyes as if at the most exquisite moment

of a very long opera, and then we are off!
without reproach and without hope that our delicate feet

will touch the earth again, let alone 'very soon.'
It is the law of my own voice I shall investigate.

I start like ice, my finger to my ear, my ear
to my heart, that proud cur at the garbage can

in the rain. It's wonderful to admire oneself
with complete candor, tallying up the merits of each

of the latrines. 14th Street is drunken and credulous,
53rd tried to tremble but is too at rest. The good

love a park and the inept a railway station,
and there are the divine ones who drag themselves up

and down the lengthening shadow of an Abyssinian head
in the dust, trailing their long elegant heels of hot air

crying to confuse the brave 'It's a summer day,
and I want to be wanted more than anything else in the world.'

Allen Ginsberg

(1926 – 1997)

*Perhaps the best known American poet of the post-World War II period, Allen
Ginsberg was a central figure in the "Beat Generation" and an important
contributor to the later Gay Liberation movement. Much of his poetry reflects
his involvement with countercultural politics and Eastern spirituality. His classic
"Howl" (which faced an obscenity trial when it was published in 1956) and
"Kaddish" combined deep emotion with iconoclasm and taboo-breaking
language. He was also a photographer and a patron and supporter of
younger writers.*

Sweet Boy, Gimme Yr Ass

lemme kiss your face, lick your neck
touch your lips, tongue tickle tongue end
nose to nose, quiet questions
ever slept with a man before?
hand stroking your back slowly down to the cheeks' moist hair soft
       asshole
eyes to eyes blur, a tear strained from seeing—

Come on boy, fingers thru my hair
Pull my beard, kiss my eyelids, tongue my ear, lips light on my forehead
—met you in the street you carried my package—
Put your hand down to my legs,
touch if it's there, the prick shaft delicate
hot in your rounded palm, soft thumb on cockhead—

Come on come on kiss my full lipped, wet tongue, eyes open—
animal in the zoo looking out of skull cage—you
smile, I'm here so are you, hand tracing your abdomen
from nipple down rib cage smooth skinn'd past belly veins, along
       muscle to your silk-shiny groin
across the long prick down your right thigh
up the smooth road muscle wall to titty again—

Come on go down on me your throat
swallowing my shaft to the base tongue
cock solid suck—
I'll do the same your stiff prick's soft skin, lick your ass—

Come on Come on, open up, legs apart here this pillow
under your buttock
Come on take it here's vaseline the hard on here's
your old ass lying easy up in the air—here's
a hot prick at yr soft mouthed asshole—just relax and let it in—
Yeah just relax hey Carlos lemme in, I love you, yeah how come
you came here anyway except this kiss arms round my neck
                              mouth open your
          two eyes looking up, this hard slow thrust this
                    softness this relaxed sweet sigh.

New York, 3 January 1974, to C. R.

Please Master

Please master can I touch your cheek
please master can I kneel at your feet
please master can I loosen your blue pants
please master can I gaze at your golden haired belly
please master can I gently take down your shorts
please master can I have your thighs bare to my eyes
please master can I take off my clothes below your chair
please master can I kiss your ankles and soul
please master can I touch lips to your hard muscle hairless thigh
please master can I lay my ear pressed to your stomach
please master can I wrap my arms around your white ass
please master can I lick your groin curled with blond soft fur
please master can I touch my tongue to your rosy asshole
please master may I pass my face to your balls,
please master, please look into my eyes,
please master order me down on the floor,
please master tell me to lick your thick shaft
please master put your rough hands on my bald hairy skull
please master press my mouth to your prick-heart

please master press my face into your belly, pull me slowly strong
        thumbed
till your dumb hardness fills my throat to the base
till I swallow & taste your delicate flesh-hot prick barrel veined Please
Master push my shoulders away and stare in my eyes, & make me bend
        over the table
please master grab my thighs and lift my ass to your waist
please master your hand's rough stroke on my neck your palm down
        my backside
please master push me up, my feet on chairs, till my hole feels the
        breath of your spit and your thumb stroke
please master make me say Please Master Fuck me now Please
Master grease my balls and hairmouth with sweet vaselines
please master stroke your shaft with white creams
please master touch your cock head to my wrinkled self-hole
please master push it in gently, your elbows enwrapped round my breast
your arms passing down to my belly, my penis you touch w/ your
        fingers
please master shove it in me a little, a little, a little,
please master sink your droor thing down my behind
& please master make me wiggle my rear to eat up the prick trunk
till my asshalfs cuddle your thighs, my back bent over,
till I'm alone sticking out, your sword stuck throbbing in me
please master pull out and slowly roll into the bottom
please master lunge it again, and withdraw to the tip
please please master fuck me again with your self, please fuck me Please
Master drive down till it hurts me the softness the
Softness please master make love to my ass, give body to center, & fuck
        me for good like a girl,
tenderly clasp me please master I take me to thee,
& drive in my belly your selfsame sweet heat-rood
you fingered in solitude Denver or Brooklyn or fucked in a maiden in
        Paris carlots
please master drive me thy vehicle, body of love drops, sweat fuck
body of tenderness, Give me your dog fuck faster
please master make me go moan on the table
Go moan O please master do fuck me like that
in your rhythm thrill-plunge & pull-back-bounce & push down
till I loosen my asshole a dog on the table yelping with terror delight to
        be loved
Please master call me a dog, an ass beast, a wet asshole,
& fuck me more violent, my eyes hid with your palms round my skull
& plunge down in a brutal hard lash thru soft drip-fish

& throb thru five seconds to spurt out your semen heat
over & over, bamming it in while I cry out your name I do love you
please Master.

May 1968

Come All Ye Brave Boys

Come all you young men that proudly display
Your torsos to the Sun on upper Broadway
Come sweet hearties so mighty with girls
So lithe and naked to kiss their gold curls
Come beautiful boys with breasts bright gold
Lie down in bed with me ere ye grow old,
Take down your blue jeans, we'll have some raw fun
Lie down on your bellies I'll fuck your soft bun.

Come heroic half naked young studs
That drive automobiles through vaginal blood
Come thin breasted boys and fat muscled kids
With sturdy cocks you deal out green lids
Turn over spread your strong legs like a lass
I'll show you the thrill to be jived up the ass
Come sweet delicate strong minded men
I'll take you thru graveyards & kiss you again

You'll die in your life, wake up in my arms
Sobbing and hugging & showing your charms
Come strong darlings tough children hard boys
Transformed with new tenderness, taught new joys
We'll lie embrac'd in full moonlight till dawn
Whiteness shows sky high over the wet lawn
Lay yr head on my shoulder kiss my lined brow
& belly to belly kiss my neck now

Yeah come on tight assed & strong cocked young fools
& shove up my belly your hard tender tools,
Suck my dick, lick my arm pit and breast
Lie back & sigh in the dawn for a rest,

Come in my arms, groan your sweet will
Come again in my mouth, lie silent & still,
Let me come in your butt, hold my head on your leg,
Let's come together, & tremble & beg.

Boulder, August 25, 1975, 4 A.M.

Night Gleam

Over and over thru the dull material world the call is made
over and over thru the dull material world I make the call
O English folk, in Sussex night, thru black beech tree branches
the full moon shone at three AM, I stood in under wear on the lawn—
I saw a mustached English man I loved, with athlete's breast and
      farmer's arms,
I lay in bed that night   many loves beating in my heart
sleepless hearing songs of generations electric returning intelligent
      memory
to my frame, and so went to dwell again in my heart
and worship the Lovers there, love's teachers, youths and poets who live
      forever
in the secret heart, in the dark night, in the full moon, year after year
over & over thru the dull material world the call is made.

July 16, 1973

Many Loves

"Resolved to sing no songs henceforth but those of manly attachment."
—Walt Whitman

Neal Cassady was my animal: he brought me to my knees
and taught me the love of his cock and the secrets of his mind
And we met and conversed, went walking in the evening by the park
Up to Harlem, recollecting Denver, and Dan Budd, a hero
And we made shift to sack out in Harlem, after a long evening,
Jack and host in a large double bed, I volunteered for the cot, and Neal
Volunteered for the cot with me, we stripped and lay down.
I wore my underwear, my shorts, and he his briefs—
lights out on the narrow bed I turned to my side, with my back to his
        Irish boy's torso,
and huddled and balanced on the edge, and kept distance—
and hung my head over and kept my arm over the side, withdrawn
And he seeing my fear stretched out his arm, and put it around my
        breast
Saying "Draw near me" and gathered me in upon him:
I lay there trembling, and felt his great arm like a king's
And his breasts, his heart slow thudding against my back,
and his middle torso, narrow and made of iron, soft at my back,
his fiery firm belly warming me while I trembled—
His belly of fists and starvation, his belly a thousand girls kissed in
        Colorado
his belly of rocks thrown over Denver roofs, prowess of jumping and
        fists, his stomach of solitudes,
His belly of burning iron and jails affectionate to my side:
I began to tremble, he pulled me in closer with his arm, and hugged me
        long and close
my soul melted, secrecy departed, I became
Thenceforth open to his nature as a flower in the shining sun.
And below his belly, in white underwear, tight between my buttocks,
His own loins against me soft, nestling in comradeship, put forth &
        pressed into me, open to my awareness,
slowly began to grow, signal me further and deeper affection, sexual
        tenderness.
So gentle the man, so sweet the moment, so kind the thighs that
        nuzzled against me smooth-skinned powerful, warm by my legs
That my body shudders and trembles with happiness, remembering—
His hand opened up on my belly, his palms and fingers flat against my
        skin

I fell to him, and turned, shifting, put my face on his arm resting,
my chest against his, he helped me to turn, and held me closer
his arm at my back beneath my head, and arm at my buttocks tender
       holding me in,
our bellies together nestling, loins touched together, pressing and
       knowledgeable each other's hardness, and mine stuck out of my
       underwear.
Then I pressed in closer and drew my leg up between his, and he lay
       half on me with his thighs and bedded me down close, caressing
and moved together pressing his cock to my thigh and mine to his
slowly, and slowly began a love match that continues in my imagination
       to this day a full decade.
Thus I met Neal & thus we felt each other's flesh and owned each
       other bodies and souls.
So then as I lay on his breast with my arms clasped around his neck and
       his cheek against mine,
I put my hand down to feel his great back for the first time, jaws and
       pectorals of steel at my fingers,
closer and stiller, down the silken iron back to his waist, the whole of
       his torso now open
my hand at his waist trembling, waited delaying and under the elastic of
       his briefs,
I first touched the smooth mount of his rock buttocks, silken in power,
       rounded in animal fucking and bodily nights over nurses and
       school-girls,
O ass of long solitudes in stolen cars, and solitudes on curbs, musing
       fist in cheek,
Ass of a thousand farewells, ass of youth, youth's lovers,
Ass of a thousand lonely craps in gas stations ass of great painful
       secrecies of the years
O ass of mystery and night! ass of gymnasiums and muscular pants
ass of high schools and masturbation ass of lone delight, ass of mankind,
       so beautiful and hollow, dowry of Mind of Angels,
Ass of hero, Neal Cassady, I had at my hand: my fingers traced the curve
       to the bottom of his thighs.
I raised my thighs and stripped down my shorts to my knees, and bent
       to push them off
and he raised me up from his chest, and pulled down his pants the
same, humble and meek and obedient to his mood our silence,
and naked at long last with angel & greek & athlete & hero and
       brother and boy of my dreams
I lay with my hair intermixed with his, he asking me "What shall we
       do now?"

—And confessed, years later, he thinking I was not a queer at first to
      please me & serve me, to blow me and make me come, maybe
      or if I were queer, that's what I'd likely want of a dumb bastard
      like him.
But I made my first mistake, and made him then and there my master,
      and bowed my head, and holding his buttock
Took up his hard-on and held it, feeling it throb and pressing my own
      at his knee & breathing showed him I needed him, cock, for my
      dreams of insatiety & lone love.

—And I lie here naked in the dark, dreaming

Arctic, August 10, 1956

Thom Gunn

(1929 –

Thom Gunn's first book of poems, Fighting Terms, *was published when
he was still an undergraduate in his native England. He immigrated to America
in 1954 to be with his lover. In spite of his long residence in California, he
has never forsaken his British roots, often rendering unconventional subject
matter in traditional, tightly controlled verse forms influenced by Auden and
Yvor Winters.*

Elegy

I can almost see it
Thin, tall, half-handsome
the thin hungry sweetness
of his smile gone
as he makes up his mind
and walks behind the barn
in his thin pointed boots
over the crackling eucalyptus leaves
and shoots himself in the head

Even the terror
of leaving life like that
better than the terror
of being unable to handle it

Though I hardly knew him
I rehearse it again and again
Did he smell eucalyptus last?
No it was his own blood
as he choked on it

They keep leaving me
and they don't
tell me they don't
warn me that this is
the last time I'll be seeing them

as they drop away
like Danny or
slowly estrange themselves

There will be no turn of the river
where we are all reunited
in a wonderful party
the picnic spread
all the lost found
as in hide and seek

An odd comfort
that the way we are always
most in agreement
is in playing the same game
where everyone always gets lost

Sweet Things

He licks the last chocolate ice cream
from the scabbed corners of his mouth.
Sitting in the sun on a step
outside the laundromat,
mongoloid Don turns his crewcut head
and spies me coming down the street.
'Hi!' He says it with the mannered
enthusiasm of a fraternity brother.
'Take me cross the street!?' part
question part command. I hold
the sticky bunch of small fingers in mine
and we stumble across. They sell
peaches and pears over there,
the juice will dribble down your chin.
He turns before I leave him,
saying abruptly with the same
mixture of order and request
'Gimme a quarter!?' I
don't give it, never have, not to him,
I wonder why not, and as I
walk on alone I realize

it's because his seven-year-old mind
never recognizes me, me
for myself, he only says hi
for what he can get, quarters to
buy sweet things, one after another,
he goes from store to store, from
candy store to ice cream store to
bakery to produce market, unending
quest for the palate's pleasure. Then
out to panhandle again,
more quarters, more sweet things.

My errands are toothpaste,
vitamin pills and a book of stamps.
No self-indulgence there.
But who's this coming up? It's
John, no Chuck, how
could his name have slipped my mind.
Chuck gives a one-sided smile, he stands
as if fresh from a laundromat,
a scrubbed cowboy, Tom Sawyer
grown up, yet stylish, perhaps
even careful, his dark hair
slicked back in the latest manner.
When he shakes my hand I feel
a dry finger playfully bending inward
and touching my palm in secret.
'It's a long time
since we got together,' says John.
Chuck, that is. The warm teasing
tickle in the cave of our handshake
took my mind off toothpaste,
snatched it off, indeed.
How handsome he is in
his lust and energy, in his
fine display of impulse.
Boldly 'How about now?' I say
knowing the answer. My boy
I could eat you whole. In the long pause
I gaze at him up and down and
from his blue sneakers back to the redawning
one-sided smile. We know our charm.
We know delay makes pleasure great.

In our eyes, on our tongues,
we savour the approaching delight
of things we know yet are fresh always.
Sweet things. Sweet things.

The Miracle

'Right to the end, that man, he was so hot
That driving to the airport we stopped off
At some MacDonald's and do you know what,
We did it there. He couldn't get enough.'
—'There at the counter?'—'No, that's public stuff:

'There in the rest room. He pulled down my fly,
And through his shirt I felt him warm and trim.
I squeezed his nipples and began to cry
At losing this, my miracle, so slim
That I could grip my wrist in back of him.

'Then suddenly he dropped down on one knee
Right by the urinal in his only suit
And let it fly, saying Keep it there for me,
And smiling up. I can still see him shoot.
Look at that snail-track on the toe of my boot.'

—'Snail-track?'—'Yes, there.'—'That was six months ago.
How can it still be there?'—'My friend, at night
I make it shine again, I love him so,
Like they renew a saint's blood out of sight.
But we're not Catholic, see, so it's all right.'

Gift

First saw him
on the street in front, in the
bar's garbage, identifying
unfinished beers and swigging
off what was left of them,
shameless and exuberant
remarking in friendly fashion
"It's a doggy dog world."
Charming error. He
had little idea of his looks
caught on a brief sill
between youthful lean times
and blowziness to come,
and too unfocused to try
hustling more than beer
and a night out of the rain.
Later, circling vaguely
the bar's deep dark inside.
"Hitched up from New Orleans,"
he said, "here, wanna feel it?"
It was already out,
pushed soft into my hand. It was
a lovely gift to offer an old
stranger
            without conditions,
a present from New Orleans
in a doggy dog world.

Peter Orlovsky

(1933 –

A key member of the "Beat Generation," Peter Orlovsky is best known for his decades-long partnership with Allen Ginsberg, whom he met when he was 21. Shortly afterwards, they exchanged vows in a San Francisco coffee shop at 3AM: "We looked in each other's eyes and there was a kind of celestial cold fire that crept over us and blazed up and illuminated the entire cafeteria and made it an eternal place."

Some One Liked Me When I was Twelve

When I was a kid in summer camp,
around 13teen & one night I lay asleep
in bunglow bed with 13teen other boys,
when in comes one of the camp councilors
who is nice fellow that likes ya, comeing to
my bed, sits down & starts to say: now you
will be leaving soon back to Flushing & I may never see you
again—but if theres ever aneything I

can do to help ya let me know, my farther is
a lawyer & I live at such & such a place
& this is my adress—I like you very much—
& if yr ever alone in the world come to me.
So I loked at him getting sad & tuched &
then years latter like now, 28, laying on
bed, my hunney-due mellon Allen sleeping next to me
—I realize he was quear & wanted my
flesh meat & my sweetness of that age—
that we just might of given each other.

April 1962, Bombay

Second Sex Experiment

PO: Allen is going to blow me till I get a good hard-on so
that I can screw him get it in him &—he takes my pants
down wile I'm typeing

AG: I'll take yr pants down wile yr typeing—

PO: ready?

AG: him him

PO: Allen puts his head against my back & arms me around the tummey, kisses my back, starts to finger my cock—I get the slight tickle—
slightley thrilled—slight thrill, slight—in my cock—almost could say
blow me

AG: I love you, & I dig the fact yr more independant—but I feel more
afraid, the contact will be broken between us—do you love me? As
long as we love each other I dont care what happens—but I dont want
to be no contact between us—

PO: I love you—he starts to go for my between legs, lays there with his
head—& breathes breaths—starts to suck my breast—my hard-on thrill
comes back—will tell him to blow me now—hope he starts to blow
me without me haveing to tell him—more sexier that way—he will see
my hard-on & start—yes thats what hes doing—I like this a lot—he
starts to move in on my cock—wants more leaway between my legs &
arm that are slightly in his way—goes up to my tits again after makeing
it on my cock again—gets up & lifts his head—on my other tit now &
breathing more fulley & sucking more deeper—down to my cock
again—lifts his head to my other side, my left to get at my breast &
now my cock—his knees on the bed, his ass up in the air facing the
celing—hear the sucking noise of his mouth on my cock—would like
to come now but—dont realey care unless I get that certain screem of
thrill love hot stream piek flow spark—my hard-on going slightly
down—he starts kissing my leg—whats he doing now—going for my
ass—I hope not I just took a crap a few minutes ago—& he came
down to same bathroom whear I was taking a crap & jerking off but
dident finish the jerkoff because he came along—now hes on my tit—
& looks with his eyes to my face, I see him out corner of my eyes

AG: Kiss me?

PO: I do for a short wile & then get back to

AG: Why dont you put the typewritter on my back then I can blow you directly?

PO: He now is in my ear—& has his hand on my head

AG: Does that feel good or am I just bugging you?

PO: No everything is fine.

AG: Feels very good, I never did this before—aneything ya want me to do?

PO: Keep blowing me

AG: Which side do you like better?

PO: Aney side thats convient for you or you like. He gets knees on the floor & tackles my cock that way—am getting hot—me think I am GOING TO FEEL HOT MORE—hard-on coming back—will I be able to come wile I am typeing—hope to god I can—come get hot pete—up & down he moves—think about girls now—who—fuck me babey—come on you spread yr cunt—allen should be bloweing harder & FASTER—a rythum—I need hes doing it now—his hand there— hes doing that now—I need—now hes after my balls with his tung— my hard-on gone down somewhat—I need faster manpower from him & suck-pull—I dont think I'll be able to come—hes got the rythum back—the beds vibratting a little—he stops I see his back & round but- tocks sticking up from the floor—he gets up

AG: I get back upon the bed. Ya got a hankerchief?

PO: Yeha—I go up to my coat on the wall & get into pocket there one for him—he on bed now with mouth on my cock—but before he did that he brought his mouth to my ass on the bed—his fingers trying to work there way into my ass hole—his mouth on my tit now—deep suck—back to my cock—he puls a hair out from between his lips—my cock hairs hes back sucking again & kinda quite down there—he moves about again

AG: Ya want to do something—

PO: Whats that?

AG: Stand over bed over the typewriter, & I'll show you something & Extradoranarry—

PO: He goes for my neck & fingers my tummey & licks his tung into my face

AG: You can type standing up a little cant ya?

PO: Sure. What ya want to do. Its dirty

AG: Are you sure?

PO: I just took a crap a cuple of minutes ago

AG: just keep typeing—I'll take care of it.

PO: He goes for water bottle & towel & after he does that wants me to sit on his face—I do

AG: I do but its too much weight for him—hes breathing too hard & has to figure how to support my weight on his face—he usses his arms—hes strugleing a little bit

AG: That feels very strange—

PO: I move my possison to sit on his chest & then he wips my cock into his mouth—hes rubbing my breasts—& streaches his legs apart, one against the wall one up near my head beside it—hes milking my tits—my hard-on slightly comming back—I realey want to come wile at typewritter

AG: Does this possission hert you?

PO: No, keep blowing me as I would like to come at type(writter)— for thats what I want to do & so you just keep bloweing & not worrey about what I do but keep yr self going bloweing & not worrey about what I do but keep yr self going bloweing me & I'll take care of this part—I would realey like to come wile at this typewritter—

AG: I would realey like you to screw me—

PO: But that would—I dont think I'll be able to come &

AG: That feels good—I dreamed a lot about that in Mareekiesh—

PO: His cock falls out of my mouth as he passing infrunt of me—

AG: But whats the realey best way to blow you—lift up—thats better

PO: He fixes the bed mattress—bends down again on bed & head on my lap starts continueing to blow me—my hard-on gone down—he cops my balls & sucks my cock with his mouth & his other arm is around my hip & hugs it—other right arm down to my foot on floor—noise of his mouth—my cock feels funney sensation—slightly annoyeing feeling—typewritter cover falls over—

AG: can you put yr feet there?

PO: ya, I can do that.

AG: okay?

PO: ya, i am still typeing—it hearts a little bit—

AG: Is there aney way to stop it?

PO: I dont know, its prittey far in.

PO: hes comming—grabs my waist & huggs me—lifts my shirt up to get to my breast—fingers my cock with his right hand—jerking me off—he came, thats good—& so fast—he must of liked it—hes holding on to my balls now & pressing his head-nose against my back—& he sighs & I feel no pain now that its over & hes still, relaxed—he coughs & says You know what, Peter—you kow that possition is like this scene—its like a Bregual*—what you think—?

PO: Yeah. He takes his cock out of my ass, gently—a ball of shit falls out on the pillow—looks like shape of chicken heart—Allen thought it was come—but no—he puts it on white paper & carries it—gets behind me & wipes my ass with underpants & krinckles my shit up to throw away—my ass feels free—& easey relaxed—now I go to bath-room—like I always do when he screws me & wash—he goes for cig— & says that felt very good—

AG: did you like it?

PO: in the beggining no—but when it was all over & the pain was gone OK & glad to see you likeing it with a smile on yr face

AG: Yeah—it was very luggoubrious & Bregual like.

1961, Tangiers

* *Peter Bruegel (1525 – 1569), Flemish painter.*

Mutsuo Takahashi

(1937 –

Friend of Yukio Mishima, Takahashi is without question Japan's foremost gay poet. He is celebrated for the sensuous detail by which he depicts life—especially gay life. To quote Robert Peters: "The incredible 'Ode,' which runs for some forty pages, is an incredible panegyric to the glorious stink of male sex."
(Translated by Hiroaki Sato.)

Myself with a Motorcycle

Motorcycle, the vehicle for long-haired young gods.
My god sports a glans-shaped jeweled crown we call a helmet,
sticks his legs with long shins into azure jeans,
puts on heavy boots adorned with many golden studs,
and dashes through the twilight of purple gods.
At the moment, midway on the stone steps behind a theatre, for
      example,
my god is in the midst of a blood-reeking conspiratorial discussion
      with other long-haired gods.
Their youthful conspiracy is too dazzling, too fragrant
for me, passing the foot of the stone steps, to clearly discern.
Below the stairs, only the god's seat made of steel gleams like a living
      thing.
I touch the motorcycle, particularly that part of its seat which was just
      glued to the ass of my god,
still retaining the ass's warmth.
My god eats Kentucky fried chicken, drinks Coca-Cola,
and from the dawn-colored slit of his beautiful ass he ejects shit.

Myself in Disguise of a Sacred Prostitute

From the face past noon in the handmirror held in my left hand
I meticulously plucked the whiskers one by one.
I shaved my eyebrows, penciled them, pouted my lips and rouged them.
I took a wig sprinkled with blue hair powder and put it on, placed a
        gold band on my forehead.
To conceal my Adam's apple, I put on a similar but wider gold band.
I put on bracelets, I put on anklets, I put on sheepskin sandals,
I put over my head a yellow-worn robe smelly from sweat,
picked teeth, spat out, chewed fragrant grass.
I rubbed questionable perfumed oil in my armpits and navel
and went out of the mirror, into a gallery of the collapsed pantheon.
Only young gods and travelers passed.
An emerald talking bird perched on an emerald tree and sang:
"You're a man. You're a man. Besides, you are old."
"On the abandoned road where gods and sacred travelers come and go,
are not all human beings miserable prostitutes?"
In the emerald evening I wailed aloud.

Ode

In the name of
man, member,
and the holy fluid,
AMEN.

There is a sunset
The world's most tragic
Therefore the most beautiful sunset
The hypersensitive skin of "time" that shifts every second
The world's rosy urticaria—against it
Towering dark, facing this way, a MAN

MAN Both his pained face, slightly looking down, on a sturdy neck
Of many muscles, of gnarled twisted sinews
And the bulges of flesh on his chest
Draped with curled hairs, each hard as wire
Are sealed in shadow's domain, indistinct

But where his powerful loins—which in a distant dazzling century
Of gold spurted Adam's healthy sons—
Join the monolithic flesh-filled crotch
The sacred center brimming with fertile power lies in the light
There in the hair, the downy grass licked, washed, cared for
Strand by strand by the gentle tongue of light
Rests dormant the beautiful flesh
Look closely: from its root to its festering wine-colored tip
It is plastered with a sheet of horrible ants of pleasure
Some coming in and out of the holes they bored
The man's expression that looked as if it did not move
Is slowly moving, invisible to the eye
Tenses into the form of wrath the two vines of blood vessels
That entwine his thick neck—
Only, the waves of pain that swell up from his dim underbelly
Move like the breathing earth, rising and falling, so slow
One cannot see it clearly
—Now, his ponderous head imperceptively tilts
And the wrinkles of pain that have caught his face like a net
Fleetingly mimic a delightfully laughing childlike face
This towering man does not have an arm, chopped at the shoulder
The lost arm, gaining the weight of gold, flows away
Horizontally in the river against a distant sunset, a salmon-colored sky
To this drifting sacred relic cling innumerable red ants
No, abominable women criers, hair covered with ash
The "pheasant weepers"
The obscene wailings of these women strike heaven
As the arm of gold moves little by little, to the west, to the west
Indifferent to the gloomy distant landscape—but
This man, blissfully suffering, sinks little by little
Sinks, and soon he will become invisible
Will leave only an earth-like vomit, like afterbirth
An ending of a great drama that was
Shall we call this a downfall?

Quo Vadis?
Where?
Where on earth are you going?
Please do not go
Please stay
For that I would kneel, I would kiss
The skin of your soles, turned moist, white, flaccid in the shoes
Smelly from the greasy socks, your feet

TOE	Your toes, rolling upward, nails storing dark-blue dirt
JAM	Let me give them passionate kisses repeatedly

The four spaces between the toes, four small darknesses infested
      with fungi
Backs of the arrogant toes, the arches clammy with sweat
The knotty ankles, the calves, the hams
Do accept
The wet admiration of my tongue and lips that climb leisurely
Above these, there are two splendid pillars
Entasis columns, cruel cracks running over them
The part further up, lost in a cloud of overwhelming fragrance,
      is invisible

GROIN   A perfumed oil factory, the darkness of its storehouse,
ODOR   and in the deeper darkness
      Inside its irregular, dusty pots, heavy perfumed oils
          undulate separately
In a vat, pomade kneaded with bamboo spatulas shines green
The perfumed oil of nard rubbed on the thighs, down to the
      shins
Of a bullfighter in a tight corset
The young smell of olive oil which the youths
Of the gymnasiums of ancient Greece
Rub on one another's naked skin, some standing, some bending
The smells of the balm, frankincense, myrrh, cinnamon of the
      mummies
That suspend the flowery death of young Egyptian nobles
The smells of the oil rubbed on a rifle, of an armory, of gasoline
The smell of heavy oil spreading rainbow-colored on the sea,
      over a sunken ship
Smell of iron, smell of iron rust, smell of solder
Smell of metal burnt off by a blowtorch
Smell of the dark of a smith's shop
Smell of the cord short-circuited late on a cold night
Smell of the lightning that struck, smell of a fire, smell of flint,
      smell of an ignitor
A power box, gunsmoke, cartridges, their smells
A coffee grinder, pepper grinder, muller, their smells
Smells of spices cramming the spice shelves
Of a spacious kitchen that the cooks guard
Clouds of spices, clouds of flowers
The suffocating smells of flowers
Grown in a greenhouse covered with a glass-paned ceiling
Milk vetch carpeting the field, a carpet of rape flowers

The alfalfa crushed by a young steed as it trots past, led by its trainer
Wood-sorrels, hare's-ears, dayflowers in the shadow, wild grasses, their
      smells
The azure coast, the perfume town of Grasse
Jasmine, violet, that grow in the fields under fierce sun
Mimosa, genista, that spew golden fire
Heliotrope, lilac, magnolia, their smells
The smell of lavender that is particularly manly
Smell of a strong perfume soaked into Grasse leather
Tanned hides hanging from a tanner's ceiling
Piles of a shoemaker's leather scraps, the strop the barber sharpens his
      razors on, their smells
The smell of the saddle, still raw, painful to the naked thighs
Smell of the young horse's wound covered irritably by blue flies
Smell of spilled blood, smell of blood plasma
Smell of a woodcutter's stout thighs a pack of wild dogs devours
Smell of the forest, smell of fallen leaves, rotting leaves
Beneath the rotting leaves, earthworms, sow bugs, centipedes, their
      smells
Smells of nuts, the acorns, honey locusts, hazels
The sunny smell of a pasania nut as it pops
Smell of bones washed brownish white by rains and winds
Smell of a tile made of the bone of a solitary desert animal
Smell of a copper thrown on a sheepskin spread on the sand
Smell of the saliva foaming around savage men's lips
Smell of the palm smelly with sweat
Smell of vagrancy, smell of an outlaw
The leather belts men wear around their waists to carry swords
The machete drawn with a flourish, its cool blue smell
Smell of the sea, smell of coppers on a littoral
Smell of navigation, sails tattered in wind and rain
Worm-eaten decks, hawsers that squeak, their smells
Smell of brine, separate routes, separate ports, their smells
Here now is London, a basement pub that smells of men
Male Britons crack traditional solemn jokes
And never smiling themselves
Puff Havana cigars clenched in their white teeth, that smell of tobacco
The man, impeccable dandies in every way
But totally indifferent to the nicotine that burns their nails, that smell
For the pleasure of a long winter hibernation, out of oblivion and dust
They take out their pipes made of rose roots from cold wastelands
Clean and polish them, their smell

Smell of roses, smell of a rose perfume, the cut tobacco moist with
    perfume
Smell of soap, smell of a bathroom
Eau de cologne, smell of lotions that smell of men
The Roko oil, the brilliantine fragrant on a young man's sideburns in a
    risqué print
Smell of freshly washed indigo
Smell of the sooty fireplace in an old mansion, smell of the fire in
    bygone days
Smell of the stove
Smell of the coal that bare chilblained hands pick and add
Smell of powdered coal, smell of the fire made in a powdered coal
    dump on a cold morning
Smell of the yawn of a young bum warming himself by the fire
Smell of hunger
Smell of the station where trains are rushed in and out
Smell of the grime in the waiting room criss-crossed with steam pipes
Smell of a cheap hotel, smell of the room for men
Smells of a prison, dormitory, army, the smell of war
Coarse khaki overcoats, military uniforms, boots, knapsacks, their smells
Smell of the blanket one pulls up with both hands to one's mouth
Smell of an army on the move, smell of a retreat, smell of reticence
Smell of a march, rain never ceasing
Rubber boots, the insides of sweaty rubber coats, their smells
Smells of puddles, smell of marshes
The ditch outside a public bathhouse at one a.m., the steam rising from
    the waste water, that smell
Smell of raw garbage rotting inexorably in a polyethylene bucket
Smell of fermented rice, smell of yeast
Inside the steamer, the smell of the warm leaven
Smell of the country sink outlet where water-hemlocks flourish
Smell of the flesh of a clam as it opens in tepid water in the sun
The finger, rotten purple, its joint bound with tough thread
Smell of the finger that crushed an insect, smell of the firefly's crushed
    tail
Elderberry bush growing in delicate shadows, smell of summer grasses,
    smell of overgrown grasses
The green snake cornered in the sun and stoned to death
Red ants swarm and lick its white belly, the smell
Above my head as I genuflect in the dizzying smell
YOU rise more and more haughtily, and tower
Your upper part, growing higher into the blue clouds
Drawn ever deeper into the middle of the clouds

To what shall I compare my god barely drowsing
In this floss of enclosing fragrant clouds?

PRICK   A sleeping baby rabbit, a resting dove with its head
or   buried under the spot where its wings cross
HEAD   A puppy, a kitten, a naked baby mouse
A leopard cub, a tiger cub, a wolf's babe
The Lion King's sleeping prince
A newborn lamb, its name: Innocento
Or Emmanuel, or again Salvador
A nursling among nurslings, a life among lives
An infant in the bedstraw of a stable
A solitary child wrapped in a radiate halo
An infant king who is offered tribute and felicitation
By stars, shepherds, and wise men, in other words, by the whole
        world
A horse stretches its neck toward the sleeping infant and neighs
As it neighs, the iron bells on its neck clank
Each of the horses that come and go along the highway has
        bells on its neck
Camel bells, mule bells, donkey bells
Bells on the ox of an ox-cart, large bells and small bells
A wayside shrine's marvelously slitted copper bell one clangs
Pulling the rope made of twined red and white ropes
A bell-shaped censer
The censer at the end of the chain an acolyte swings to the
        priest's litany
The censers being swung in the thousand chancels of a
        thousand sanctuaries on the *duplex I classis*
On a bright summer evening the rain goddess wets the dome of
        a great temple with her tongue
The mosque of Cairo, the mosque of Tripoli, the mosque of Tunis
Hagia Sophia of Constantinople
The font of Hagia Sophia
The Tower of Babel from which the inheritors of the earth
        scattered in the four directions
The giant totem pole that monkeys climb
The giant birth-stone a thousand blind men cling to and lick
Fire worshippers' fire tower, the Oloth altar that scorches heaven
The Altar of Heaven, the yin-yang platform, the astrological
        tower of the doctors from the East
The dome of a great observatory, the armillary sphere
A planetarium which enwraps a faultless starry sky

An advertising tower, the barber's candy stick that turns, an artery and
    vein entwining it
The scarlet knob on a bridge post, the marble statue of an angel near
    the bridge
A castle fair on the hill, towers soaring in a closed city of stone
A watchtower where a night guard paces back and forth, rattling his
    gun and sword
The tower in a fort, the tower in a monastery, the tower in the King's
    castle
With an innocent man incarcerated, the tower of a ruined castle rises in
    deep silence
A ghastly moon out of the clouds gives half of it to light, half of it to
    shadow—
A marshy zone where fog rises every night—unsheathing itself from
    the whirling flows of fog, a tower
A finely crackled tower, a tower covered with green ivy
A tower in the wasteland, a tower in the forest, a tower on the cliff, a
    lighthouse washed by waves
Pharos in ancient times burning raw olive
Flames itself bright, and only itself, in the dark sea and the dark night—
In the morning sea, parting waves churning white, a prideful figurehead
Sharply slicing apart the blowing ocean wind
Continues to dream of a glittering haven far beyond the ocean route—
Sails swollen with wind, a ship swollen with sails
A battleship, a destroyer, a landing craft
A submarine moving through the depths of heavy water
Launched incessantly upward from its nose, torpedoes
The shark-shaped torpedo, the torpedo-shaped shark
A shark, a dolphin, a sperm whale, the big fish that swallowed the
    prophet
Jerked up with a cruel hook, a fish with a gleaming belly
Taken out of the fish belly, twitching entrails wet with blood
A young fishmonger's obscene hands soiled with sticky blood
Gleaming fish moving through the brine a thousand fathoms deep
His nude body closely draped with corpses of noctilucae
A man swims over-arm toward a boat in the offing
A slimy fur seal, a sea lion, an otter
Caught in an aurora, a seal barks on the floe
Heaven's inverse tower peering out of the unknowable heavens
God's fingers, the miraculous fingers that give up blessings
Tathagata's light-emanating fingers towering at the limits of heaven
The thumb that the *imperator* with a sharp-eyed eagle perched on his
    stout shoulder

Raises ponderously to signal "Strike!"
The fingers for the signals a catcher with powerful hips makes between
       his thighs
The stonemason's sinewy thick fingers, the cooper's chapped fingers
A young *yakuza*'s severed small finger, discolored in a small cloth
The philanderer's hooked, hunting finger
The toes arched toward the horizon of pleasure and death
Stubborn toes, willful toes, brazen, shameless toes
The shanks of Atlas indurate under the weight of heaven, the pillars of
       heaven
Marble pillars that supported the gabled roof of a pantheon
Under the blue sky, columns lie shattered, now with nothing to support
The pillars of the Senate, pillars of a gallery surrounding a plaza, pillars
       of the Colosseum
The Colosseum's arena, the bottom of a silence guarded by thousands
       of cruel eyes
The stiffened legs of contestants who yell and clash
On the dry ground, a chopped, heavy shank
In the swirling dust of a bullring, a mad blind bull
A cattle herd in a corral, a leaping bull, a bull-headed bull, a violent bull
       in rut
Battling bulls grinding their arched horns together
A drinking horn ornamented with gold work
The unicorn, the rhinoceros' unseemly horn
The velvety antlers that a young stag in early spring rubs against a
       stump itchingly
The malevolent interglacial horse, now extinct
A rushing horse, a bronco, an impetuous, spirited, rearing horse
A knight in the saddle, chest stuck out, armor glistening
An advancing knight, a retreating knight, a triumphant knight
Neck pierced, a knight topples down
The sword a knight holds over his head, a sword that has been given a
       benediction, an emerald dagger
A decorative sword inlaid with agate and jade
A spear pierces a pliant youth, its spearhead upright
The red hot blade, the cutting edge of a sword, the blade of a hatchet,
       the blade of a kitchen knife
That are hammered by turns on the blacksmith's anvil
A soldering iron pulled out of charcoal fire and glowing fire
A burning log one pulls out of the stove, a torch in the dark
One sucks in, and the cigar glows
Dawn-colored ivory, the mammoth's elegantly arched tusk
A ruddy-faced craftsman dexterously

Pulls a long iron tube out of the molten oven
And balling up his cheeks, blows a bottle shape
A lamp in a mountain hut, a hanging lamp in a boat house, a dark
      lantern
The chimney of the lamp that boys of Harlem used night after night
To burn with its oily-smelling flames the hair of the parts they were
      bashful about
The glowworm that goes back and forth through the dark marrow of a
      tree
A silkworm, a larva, a magnificent maggot sated on rotten meat
A slug leaves a gleaming trail, weaving ahead
A viper with its fierce head, a rattlesnake, a slow python
Under a caressing hand a cobra raises its sinuous head for love
A tamed Indian tortoise, the tortoise's leathery head
A leathery elephant, the elephant's leathery trunk, a Goblin's long nose
A hooked nose, a roman nose, a snotty nose
A boxer's squashed nose, a nose dripping with a cold
A purplish nose ulcerous from liquor
A nose sniffing for the wine smell from a distant wine cellar
A wine jar in the wine cellar's inmost part, a milk jar, a jar of honey
A pigskin sack one hooks to the wall to ripen cheeses in
A leather sack of wine a thirsty traveler
Takes down from his horse, holds up in both hands, puts his mouth to,
      and guzzles from
Peach-colored stuffed meat dangling in the dark of a butcher shop, a
      half-rotten ham
An abundantly seasoned, well salted, purplish-black sausage
As they sway greenbottles fly about noisily buzzing—
Salt pork on the carving board, a pickled cucumber, a pickled eggplant
An apple baked with rum, a peach baked with cognac
A leaden *pidan* that ripened in mud, a heavy egg boiled too long
A light peach-colored nesting egg that one makes a hole in with a
      gimlet and slurps from
A goose egg that has an erotic picture on it, painted with a delicate
      gold-covered Chinese brush
A duck egg, a turkey egg, a guinea hen's mottled egg
Fox-colored fried cookies with plenty of milk and yolk
In the crowd of an open-air market one fondly remembers
A fat elephant of a man, all smiles
Sprinkles sweet sugar, top and bottom
With his huge hand rubbed on his apron—
A red mullet seasoned with pepper, *wijnruit,* onion, and mustard
Heliogabalus' conger eels fed and fattened

On the live flesh of young slaves handpicked for brawn and beauty
A carp fried whole, a lamprey cooked whole
Cod roes, sea bream roes, roes of a roach crisscrossed with blood vessels
Pomegranates that have exploded on each branch, showing blood-
        colored insides, exploded heads
A head that ripened to the full and dropped from the neck, blood
        spurting
A criminal's head a wrestler wrenched off, his arms bulging with muscles
A rebel's head rolling, chagrined, under the guillotine
A boxer's neck with swollen veins, a philosopher's neck, Agrippa's head
A neck with two or three lines of soiled wrinkles, the lightly dyed
        neckskin
The head of a lion bearing his incisors, the head of a foaming horse
        near death, a bull's bloodied head
The neck of a wild goose flying over reed marshes, a drake's blue neck
        swiftly erected
The neck of a proud fighting cock, the neck of a cassowary, a chicken's
        neck rolling on the floor of a poultry shop
A flower that blossomed to the full and dropped with its calyx, the head
        of a flower
And since we're on flowers, the bud of a pallid, ponderous lily
The bud of a cape jasmine, buds of a purple magnolia, an evergreen
        magnolia
An anemone about to open, moist with dew
A tulip about to open, a water lily about to open
A creeping myrtle hanging from vines, a trumpet creeper
An akebi torn purple, hanging from heaven
Duped by the sweet-sour fragrance, from somewhere
Slim-waisted yellow jackets gather—
A mango, papaya, durian with a strong aroma
A banana gives off fragrance when peeled
The coconut one holds with both hands in a cool shade and pleasantly
        drinks its juice from
The tight, bumpy head of a native drinking from a coconut
Novel fruits brought over across the salt-fragrant oceans
Mandarin oranges guarded by Hsi Wang Mu's ladies-in-waiting
Litchi nuts with a taste of tears, which messengers carry a thousand
        miles, whipping relays of horses
Monstrous nuts that speak a human tongue in a barbaric Hsi-yu country
In the morning field, a dew-drenched, muddy melon
A watermelon, its red inside peering out of the crack made when it
        dropped on the road
A butchered infant's head, its wet brains peering out

Inside a sleeping infant sleeps an adult
Life in a sleeping adult, death in life
Glory equal to ruin, medicine equal to poison, good equal to evil
Temptation equal to salvation, salvation equal to temptation
Adam on the sixth day of creation, equal to the fallen archangel
The terrifying judge on the day of judgment, equal to one waiting at
      the bottom of hell's darkness
Ruler of the lights and shadows of mountains, rivers, and deserts
Of oceans and firmament, cities and countries
The one pierced by the arrows, *oratio jaculatoria,* of prayers and grudges,
      of ice and fire
Shot by the multitudes that merely repeat births and deaths
In the four directions, scanned with narrowed eyes, hand shading the
      light
To the limits of the earth where horse hoofs swirl up dust
The only word, the only law, the only principle—
Before YOUR dazzling self entwined with the vines
Of our adorations and curses, I shall prostrate myself
I shall weep, I shall plead, I shall entreat

        There, I caught you
        Lovely male rabbit
        Held down in my hands, you bounce
        With vigor, like a spring
        Like the tip of a fountain pressed under the hand of a
            naughty boy
        Like a balloon a young stallkeeper pumps hydrogen into
        And then makes squeak on a festival night
        Like a carp the diver in the cold February water
        Has gripped with both hands
        I caught you, in the dark of a newsreel theater
        In the forest of human columns in a steam-filled Turkish
            bath
        In the cloud of aromas in a public men's room
        In the sweat-reeking throngs on a crowded train
        Wait, agile male rabbit
        Hopping down the stairs to the basement country
        That suggests the river bank in Wonderland
        Where are you running away to?
GROPETERIA   Underneath is a forest of miracles
        Off the busy street, in a cheap basement movie house,
            behind its empty front seats
        The wordlessly stirring forest is a forest of flesh

What curse has changed these people
Into abominable trees?
Oh, these saint-like, apostle-like people
Standing uneasily, unable to move!
To the eye that has entered the dark abruptly from light
These thronging people loom merely black
But as they sway like aristae swaying
Almost imperceptibly on a windless, full moon night
Their heads, their shoulders
Blurred by the reflections of white images
Cast on the screen, are like the blessed signs
To tell holiness by, the dazzling auras
The shadows spout black sweat
Feigning indifference, but the moment the backs of hands casually
        groping
Assure each other they turn with the alacrity
Of aspen leaves in the wind, and the hunting fingers
Swim into the spaces between fingers, the parts where thin webs are
And in the end tightly grip each other
Hand, the first signal exchanged, separates from hand
Falls upon the stirring bulge in the cloth of the other's pants
And welcomes, fondles, loves
The sugar lump which, licked by ants of pleasure
Crumbles from its top in drivels blended with formic acid
The nest of yellow jackets full of holes
Packed with flabby delicious wasp babies
Around the encounter of two martyrs, the other saints
Happily make a firm, protecting, human fence
In which the two exchange love where a moment is an eternity
Here in the catacombs
There are no burning candles, shining icons, or glittering ritual objects
But people gather here from crossroads, from networks of labyrinths
With the same sufferings, same wishes, same longings
Their other secret meeting place is the place closest to the skies
After climbing and climbing many turns of stairs
A cheap movie house with a low ceiling that touches one's head
Its lavatory—the back of a building is all that's visible from its small
        window
From there, can't one go to heaven's lavatory along the road of an
        invisible rope?
At this very moment, in heaven's lavatory, among young angels
Are YOU dreamily jerking off?
Here, to climb is to descend

To descend, to climb
No, to climb and to descend are one
As in the Eleusinian mysteries

TURKISH   Come now, wait, naughty child
EMBASSY   What's ahead of this hole is a sacred basement Turkish
           bath
One pushes in the steamy glass door like the entrance
To limbo, and on hell's languidly descending slope
Faces blurred like soles of feet all turn to look
Noses and ears gone flabby, and near their amorphous eyes
Dizzying blind mirrors are plastered
One looks back, and there
At the focal distance of the lens of steam, a crowd of distorted ghosts
The white steam that leaks from a pipe rusted red spurts up
Hissing, hits the wall, changes its direction
All at once reaches the ceiling
And exhausted, drips, drips, drips
And drips onto the flowing floor where sitting flatly
Like the lion Heracles the bathhouse god once kept
Mouths smellier than the latrine, darker than a grave, agape
Tongues bent like a carpenter's square, just as sea anemones wait for a
           small fish
Some wait for the arrival of a lively male rabbit
As for those standing, each one of them
Like a sick frog, has a pale swollen underbelly
Leathery pointed elbows, dirty corned heels
Several long idle hairs growing from a mole near the shoulder
Buttocks, fleshless, skin hanging loose like a balloon with the air gone
Rheum exuding from the mucous suppurating corners of the eyes
The eyes sidewise ogle a neighbor
And then again feign utter unconcern
These garbage bags of prurience and muck
Jostle and push one another in the chamber
And from the heads of their larvae dangling in white hair
Toyed with by the finger tips of absurdly long mummy fingers
Drips withering, smelly juice
Which threads down sluggishly like the sticky stuff in fermented
           soybeans
Should, by mistake, a boy who knows nothing
Wander in, swiftly
Vines would slide out of these garbage bags
And swaddle the boy's flesh

The vines would oh ever so lightly transport it
To the pinnacle of delight, and at the pinnacle of blazing joy
The boy's face would easily avalanche to ugly old age
And so he too would become an insidious one among the crowd of
      insidious *pretas*
In the boiling Tapana Hell
The saint's phrase, "the community of hatred"
Is appropriate for this hateful crowd
Verily, here there's no love of any kind
But it is also true that they are yearning for
A love like enwrapped light
A love enrolled in a cocoon of gentleness
Like that of the stars of the Twins
How, and where, have the tips of the lights
These travelers protected as they wandered in the land of love
Gone awry in storms of evil?
Saints, pity these people

TEA   The hole also leads to the public men's room
HOUSE   underground
          The spiral staircase turns twice, turns three times
    Excreta, semen, tar of tobacco, sodden, rotting emotions
    From them, furiously, rise the scents—in their midst
    In the drifting five-colored clouds, in the mist of the five
          skandha, one stands and strains one's eyes
    The four sides of the cloud-mist painful to the eye are the
          concrete walls of grief that nightly suck the dew—
    On the walls, ideograms of grief jostling, rising to the ceiling,
          psalms of grief
    —One of them:

Romance of the Rose

Budding rose, rose with everted petals, dew-laden rose
My rose-shaped love, my god
Where have you gone, leaving me, abandoning me
Abandoned, forgotten, I have become an idle grave
My love, asking for you, my god, looking for you
I have gone past many crossroads, but I have not found you
I am exhausted, both soul and flesh
I pray, you whom I love will pity me
Descend from heaven like a flood of light and fill me—
My grave, my throat, down to my stomach

Envoy

Wanted: A Young person. I would do anything.
My age uncertain. Please get in touch.

At the end of swirling choruses of innumerable ideograms and
      innumerable psalms
Is a sacred door to the two holiest places, two shitting places
One pushes in the door, squats before the john, and there before one's
      eyes is the sacred hole
Wanting to see beyond it the light of paradise, or else the darkness of
      hell
One puts one's eye to it, and as if to pierce the eye, a thing thrusts out
One looks again: a red hot flesh-column, its tip flushed with anger
A drop, hungry for love, a trembling transparent bead of tear
Overcome with pity, one opens one's mouth in the shape of O, wraps it
      with one's tongue
And the flesh, the spearhead, gathering strength, thrusts out and out
Soon the taut flesh bursts, melts away
And the visitor from the other side, a god, dies
Now the one on this side stirs
Becomes a god, visits beyond the hole the wet hot darkness
Becomes wrapped by the darkness, squeezed and rubbed by the
      darkness, climbs to the top
And the god this side, too, has at once a headlong fall
Two columns of deity leave each other, and only the hole remains,
      black
Verily, praise be to the hole into which one peers, which is peered into—
Through the hole that makes two solitudes one
Two shitting places one, the public men's room leads to the men's room
      of a gymnasium
Leads to the men's room of a fish market, a seamen's school, the self-
      defense forces, a prison
A dormitory, a police academy, and a police booth
Thus one would go through the peep-hole of the public men's room
Sneak into the men's room of a police booth, hold a cop from behind
Tie up his hands on his back, take off his belt, pull down the zipper
Drop his pants, hug his hips tight
And make him arch back with pleasure, make him groan, writhe
And die in spasms—oh all those young, sturdy cops
Even among them, among those thousands and thousands of illusory
      cops
YOU are not found

the   Night, with downy hair trembling the color of gold, embraces
PRICK,   A pure sleep, a pure spirit, a pure substance
again   For example, pure gold, silver, iron ore
      Light dug out of the dark earth: diamond
      Muddy crystal columns, amethyst, garnet
      A pure idea, a pure poem, a pure death
      Its innocent mimesis
      Like the soft roe which, taken out of the pliant belly
      Of a leaping male salmon gleams a rainbow color
      Like the corpse of a drowned boy rising from the water
      In the arms of sorrowful water nymphs
      Like the ancient bronze statue of a god which the wordless
           divers
      Tie to a rope and haul up from the bottom of the sea
      You, glistening-wet, inert
      Keep falling, or keep climbing
      Into a heavier sleep, into a deeper sleep—
BUSH   Surrounding a sleeping, parentless, infant brother, and shining
      Are his elder sisters—like their lice-infested hair
      Surrounding you in sleep, and shining
      Are a water nymph of the sea, a water nymph of the river
      Water nymphs of the marshes, of the waterfall, of the spring,
           their hair
      The hairs of the sea that waver as the tides move
      Rockweed, kelp, thick-haired codium, gulfweed
      Various duckweeds, in bright fresh water
      A flock of reeds at the estuary quivers delicately
      When ebbing tides cry out in the evening sun
      A marshy zone where a murderous felon escaped
      A thicket of ferns where a phallus, rotted purple, lies abandoned
      A field of bamboo grass, a field of sedge,
      A neatly mowed lawn
      A well-groomed brushwood fence
      On a moonlit night, a farm hand riding a donkey sidesaddle
      Plays the flute, passes by a field of sweet-smelling sugar cane
      A reindeer fawn, left behind by its mother
      Sad-eyed, sniffs its way over the steppe
      Hungry hyenas roam the savanna
      A wounded lion hides in a thicket of tall grass
      A hot wind passing through the thicket
      Fans out burnt grasses, insects, and the shrill smell of blood—
      A hedgerow of roses where a snake hides, a bramble of thorns

On the cool inner wall of a well in the country moss thrives
A green forest in fragrant May
In the soft sun that filters through the trees
Students on the wrestling team, sitting back to back
Arms hooked, legs stretched
Push and pull, by turns, to strengthen abdominal muscles
Oh, how they resemble those making love—
One summer day, and the cool foliage of a honeysuckle
In which two cute boys loved
Each other, cooing like two doves
In the heat of the day, Indian travelers, like persons in meditation
Rest with eyes closed in the shade of a linden
There's a yogurt vender with Indian cotton wound around his head—
There's a cow sacred to the gods, relaxing leisurely, four legs tucked
       under its body—
Brats playing at soldiers
Hide in bushes of plume goldenrod, stiff goldenrod, wasteland aster—
The day when the inner sides of one's thighs become sweaty, while
       marsh wrens jar
A golden wheat field—crawling into it
A young man makes a blushing boy play with him
The boy is moved, his heart beating like a fire bell—
July's gentle green paddies, paddies of rush
On a rafter, premonitions of a storm make a swallow chick tremble—
       the down on its neck
On a wind-howling night, heaths on the slope abruptly turn pale
A stormy forest, a shadowy forest, the King of the Wood's forest
—Here again the season of a fragrant forest
The demons' metropolis, the forest with rows of giant trees that stab
       heaven
During the day, young mothers pushing baby carriages
Grandmothers plying knitting needles, girls reading
Mischievous children in short pants, gentle lovers
Fill a corner—a heartwarming sight—
Which, as dusk sets in, reveals the other face of Janus
And in the shadows of trees, around the fence of roses, men begin to
       loiter
Their eyes flare, twinkling in the dark
Like the phosphorescence around a bone on a rainy night
These blue phosphorescent lights, sluggishly flaring
Draw large slow circles
And, each turning into viscous lime, pull each other closer
The hunter and the hunted—the movements of the two circles

Gradually slow down and finally stop
The phosphorescent lights that have become one, still smoldering
In due time leave somewhere
Two a.m., three a.m.
The forest still fragrant, circles still drawn
And soon the eastern clouds whitening

PRICK   A foundling wrapped in gentle feathers
and   The she-wolf with the twins, Romulus and Remus
BALLS   Acala the god of fire attended by Kimkara and Cetaka
Tathagata flanked by his warriors
A cannon with its two wheels
A rocket launcher equipped with two hangars—
From which the deaths of men will be recorded in a giant log
        of the space age
Are launched one after another—
A carriage with two impetuous horses
The sacred triangle, Ugolino weeping with his starved sons
Youngest prince Okuninushi carrying sacks on his back
BALLS   Bag of wrinkled leather as old as the world
A bag of tears, a bag of placer gold, a bag of sorrows of pure gold
A heavy purse of supremely soft deerskin
Filled out with jingling gold coins
Wrinkles at its mouth collected and tightly tied
A brocaded bag with flints in it
A terrifying matchbox crammed with dangerous matches
An amulet bag, a sachet, a silk napkin with a famous incense
        folded in it
On Christmas Eve, Santa Claus flies through the aurora
His cloth sack full of goodies
Decorating the four corners of an old leather map, the wind
        gods with their windbags
Momotaro's waist pouch bulging with delicious millet dumplings
Seasonal laborers looking for new jobs
Tramp along the dusty road, shoulders burdened with canvas bags
In a boxing gym, a boy attacks and sways a punching bag
Two weights, a balance
Hermes' snake-coiling balance with hefty gold lumps in both pans
In the golden year of a bumper crop, wine barrels are laid
Solidly filling the dim basement cellar
One puts in a ladder, goes down
And loses one's foothold, blunted by the mist of sweet-sour
        smell—

One peers in, and the oil in the jar wavers slimily
Tangled by spiders' slime, an endplate exudes
White dregs from its crack, of a sturdy barrel of Vino de Jerez
An iced-over pond on the mountaintop
On a bitterly cold night, the pond keeper spikes his fierce pick in
And the gallant water, spouting out as light
Jumps over the icicle-hung watergate, and comes down shrieking—
A frozen dragon egg, salmon roe embossed with blood vessels
In the water, a hyacinth bulb embossed with purple veins
The narcissus, the crocus, the saffron with their pinkish bulbs
A bunch of grapes, ripe and heavy, mulberries ripe in a foliage
A dew-laden cluster of genista flowers
A flower cluster of wisteria, paulownia flowers heavy with last night's
      rain
Drooping ears of millet moving in the wind, golden ears of rice in
      October
The deep sea that nourishes pearls, fish eggs laid on laver brushwood
A dragnet at the bottom of dark water, heavy before it is drawn up
A thunderhead, a cloud pregnant with light, a raincloud enfolding a
      whole town
An uninhabited house on a stormy day, the hideout of a murderer
A fortress with its drawbridge lifted, the miracle palace concealing
      villains
The closed Pentagon, the silent G.P.U. headquarters
In a wasted village, a towering belfry
Where for joy, or for sorrow
Innumerable bells of yore are ringing—
A blast furnace, a retort, a percolator
A thermal power plant in the folds of the mountains, a highly fragrant
      bread oven
The pot-maker's oven, in the depths of its fire masterpieces ripening
On a stormy night a thrush's nest thumps down to the ground,
      clamorous chicks and all
A mischievous child pulls out from under a tree root
A trapdoor spider's nesting bag, with the spider squirming in it
Sloshily moving, a rubber waterpillow
Folding on a rainy day and opening when it's clear, the pine cone
A slow rhinoceros with straggling hair, the leathery rhinoceros the
      leather bag
When it looks as if it's moving, it's quite still
And when it looks still, it's moving—a loose leather-made ball
Folded in a well-tanned, gentle sheepskin, a thick book of wisdom
As an infant, tiptoe, touches with its lovely hand

A loaded cluster of grapes wet with morning dew
As a forbidding mountain exorcist, whose traveling robe is of hemp
Worries and rustles his rosary of coarse beads in his terrifying hands
So one worries the balls in one's hand
              Kisses the child wrapped in the wrapping cloth
FORESKIN   And with the tongue tip sharpened like a needle, everts
              the wrapping cloth
A bandage wound tightly round and round the ring finger
The bandages for an abscess, the bandages rolling up a fireman burned
    all over
The bandages that wrap the invisible man, the bandages with a
    mummified boy-king sleeping in them
The white cover-cloth a leper has pulled over himself, from head to toe
The flowering stalk of a butterbur, a peapod, skin-covers of a bamboo
    shoot
A miscanthus roll, a taffy in a bamboo leaf, a butterball wrapped in
    cellophane
A hat, the Pope's miter, a cardinal's hat, the hood for a child in the snow
    country
The chef's somewhat grimy white toque
The K.K.K. hood, socks, a rubber thimble
A rubber glove everted like a pelt of gelatin
A god's glove that has fallen from heaven toward the sea of chaos
A turban, a calpac, the hood of the Eskimo parka
Roofs rising in the Kremlin, in rows as if in a fairy tale
In the Kremlin, from the balcony
Soviet elders wave to May Day crowds in Red Square
All in uniform caps
At Buckingham Palace, guards swagger in bearskins
Pericles' helmet, Napoleon's hat
The Pohai Emperor's hat, the Egyptian priest's headdress
The Old Blossomer's cap, Mr. Ebisu's cap
The fearful shoes, the shoes that, once put on, can't be removed
The rubber boots worn by a young cock in the fish market
The riding boots made to fit the legs closely
Each time the rider walks its spurs clack, clack
A hill-fresh yam wearing a maxicoat
A wandering yakuza's slightly soiled cape
A man rolled in a mattress carried by thugs to be dumped in the river
One unhooks the beltless, pulls the zipper
And recklessly pulls down the pants
A gaiter unwound swiftly, the leather chaps
A shutter pulled down with a rattle, a curtain, a double-leaf louver door

Concealing a man, panting, his hairy shins showing, a surgical intern in
      white
A noncommissioned officer's cap pulled down to the eyes, his uniform
      well-creased
The armor hiding the young blond knight, his Lordship
On a morning when each exhaled breath visibly turns into steam,
      white misty droplets
An autorepairman's one-piece workwear
The zipper extending down its stained cloth from neck to crotch
When one pulls it down in one breath
There, vividly, jumps out the young flesh, flushed with cold—
The leaping pink flesh wrapped in a lobster shell
The pelty diving suit, a suede suit
Skinned with a stone and bloody, a wild animal pelt
An antelope, a wolf, a coyote, their pelts
The membrane that wraps the bloody heart of a wild animal
The membrane of the morning haze that wraps the bloody daybreak
When one rolls up the haze, the gossamer tent
                Soaked with morning dew is the refreshing sun
CHEESE   Brilliant scum around the sun
                Corona, halo, ring around the eclipsed sun
On the triumphant soldier's forehead, a hoop of young laurel, olive and
      myrtle branches
A crown for breaking blockades, a citizens' crown, a naval crown, a
      crown on the castle wall
The ecliptic, the headband, that holds the celestial globe at an angle
The equatorial belt, heaven's band of animals, its twelve palaces
Saturn's double rings, the sash if Iris the rainbow goddess
The turquoise pectoral of Tutankhamon the boy king
The pectoral of gold plates that shine in many layers
Adjective, adverb, and again adverb that adorns the adverb
Dazzling rhythms around true poetry
Appoggiaturas that hold on to the *Idee* of a great symphony
Gentle compassion around true strength
Thoughtfulness, delicacy, salt of the earth
Ashes that dye the brows on Ash Wednesday
Ashes of the hemp ropes burnt on the felicitous morning of the
      election of a new Pope
Paste perfume, balsam, musk, ambergris
Cheese the northerners stir and ripen in goatskin bags
Honey congealed, fragments of a shell on which glue was kneaded
An island of mew gulls
The birds nesting along the round rim of the rocky isle

Fly away north leaving the rock mountain
Encircled by a necklace of dry white bird shit—
A white town cradling a bay, a full set of false teeth
A round archipelago, a ring of coral reefs—now, the tongue's violent
    storm
It about to lap up the whole atoll, look
When the tongue slurps past

CREVASSE   The furrow opens joyfully, the furrow leading to the
and   cord
CHORDEE   A string twisting together innumerable gold fibers of
                  pleasure
An electric cord through which run a thousand amperes of joy
A Japanese lute's resonating string, a "demoncalmer's" trembling
    bowstring
A purling stream of groans, a gleaming channel marker
A quaking arc of light, a platinum sheet of rain, a silver blind
Lightning, a road arrested in lightning
A bright sea line, an unmarked sea boundary
A horizon fringed by light
From over an invisible line, on horseback, on camelback
Or on foot, new toiling races
Emerge, one after another—
The most sensitive barometer thread
The breathtaking galactic belt
Over a dizzying gorge a taut suspension bridge
And again, the sway of the tongue
Provokes around the furrow a chorus of roars from the millet grains of
    pleasure
The sun pours its light on a single plate
In the bullring, and in the arena
Seeing blood the spectators resound in fury
The faithful congregate in the Vatican on Easter
School children at the command, "Line up for exercises!"
A thousand soldiers on review, at the moment of "Present arms!"
A thousand black slaves on the boy-king's august visit
The tongues of barnacles swing in unison at each move of the tide
On the late summer sea a thousand ripples, a thousand staysails
A thousand fragments of the evening sun on the lake—oh YOU
Please stick your praiseworthy head out of the shattering water—
A thousand zelkova leaves all sway at once
A flock of starlings fly up clamorously
In the United States of America, on Independence Day

And in the Soviet Union, on Revolution Day
Planes in a large formation converge, scatter, and then again converge
On the belt of a cultured-pearl factory hurry billions of pearls...

	Eightfold camellia that flowers on my tongue full of love
	Droplets of honeydew that collect at the tip of a petal
	Drops of costly perfumed oil that tremble on the alembic
FORECOME	Thrust forward by thoughts of tender love, I press my lips
and	To the camellia, to the alembic, to the wide-mouthed jar
COME	Joyous glitter
	That spouts and goes down my throat into hell

Frothy honey liquor that brims over the wide-mouthed pot
And spills along the shapely furrow, leaving a gleaming trail
Way beyond the seas of waves tossing in winter storms
Ferocious barbarians of an unknown country
Brewed and stored it through seasons of lasting fog and hail
The men who brewed it are gutsy and rough
But the liquor that was born is smooth and gentle to the tongue—
The sacred water that wells up on Oceanus' purifying island
And is carried in the beak of a sapient dove
To Olympus, to the lips of the gods
Dr. Faustus' mercury, the spirit of the mercury-colored earth
The water that courses through the dark underground paths
A deep well one crackles by dropping a bucket on a dark night
A sudden spout in a winter park
The smoke a rocket spews
Viscous fumes from a volcano
Lava that dribbles down toward the mountain foot
Time that drips, a clepsydra
An avalanche, a glacier going down
Frozen waterfalls, icicles, frost columns
Firefly's saliva to feed its larvae
Dragon's slobber, snake's tears, slug's path
Saint James' way, the milky river made when heaven's giant vat was
     overturned
In heaven, Ganymede the beautiful boy coyly pours nectar
From a wide-mouthed *krater*
A shooting star, a shower of the starry host
Billions of well-washed pearls
Billions of incessant arrows
Sidelong glances, a row of arrows
Darts of light, arrows of words
Love God's arrows that escape the mouth of a boy in love

A krim namah….
A swarm of honey bees, the sharp spring messenger the *Kokila* bird
Light, Holy Spirit, the tongue of a flame going down noisily
A delighted spring, a joyful stream
Touched by light, Persephone's water cries out happily
At midnight, a water-surprise
On a festival night, fireworks
A sudden visit
Brightly between the thighs, angels
The Word, what is eternally sonlike, overflows
Cheerfulness, innocence, directness comes forth
But hold it, hold it
Frowning, lips closed
And repeat over and over
Making no sense, the changes of a verb:
I will *not* fly
I *will* fly
I fly
When I fly
If I flew
Fly
Let me fly
Let's fly!

GET	Childhood dream of flying through space
YOUR	Tom Thumb riding a goose
ROCKS	Eleven princes who turned into swans
OFF	Clever kids lifted to a star

Star-shaped confetti
Confetti, alfeloa shots
Shots to blind the enemy in a snowball fight
Bow-and-arrow fight, Lord Protector of Bows and Arrows,
arrows numbering eighty thousand
Hundreds and thousands of stones flipped from a catapult
An artillery, an anti-aircraft gun, machine gun strafe like
hailstones
In a kids' war, a shower of pebbles
A knapsack hurled off
Textbooks thrown out, cards
Heaven's jewelry box thrown out
Angels who flew away
Heaven's forces on birds' wings
Hell's army on bats' membranes

A great space war that weaves through the stars
A great formation that falls burning
Dandelions parachute
Pollen that flies up in the wind
Golden kerria roses that scatter in the wind
Kerria King's generous treat
Cakes scattered, bags scattered to the crowd
Scattering large coins, small coins
Scatter, scattering away
Rolling up like a fetus
Headfirst, headlong
Heavy, lonesome, fall!

BALLAD Ah, where are they?
for the In what netherworld
LONG-DEAD Is that strange soldier who one flaming night of air raid
BOYS Picked me up
And pressed his cheek to mine?
As he picked me up
My young cheeks rubbed against the thighs of his soldier pants
And hurt pleasantly
And where are
Those handkerchiefs hung from the hips
Of the drafted students who went past me
Turning back, again and again
To see me playing with mud?
Those young fishermen
Who on starry nights, in the ship-carpenter's hut
Taught us the suffocating pain of dirty stories?
Those railway men
Out of whose faded, dark-blue work clothes
Bruised youth peered?
And yet, where are they?
Where are the roses of yesteryear?

Ah, where are they?
Under what sky
Are those cruel upper graders
Wearing shorts, knees showing?
Those bullies who on the way home from school
Ambushed me in the shrine wood
And sank me
In fond dizzying noseblood?

And where is
That junior high school gymnast
Who did a giant swing, turned round and round
Not deigning to glance at me
An admiring, spellbound schoolboy?
Or those vagrant kids who stole
The black puppy I loved so?
Mother went and pleaded with them
And obediently they returned it—their sad eyes?
And yet, where are they?
Where are the lilies of yesteryear?

For those kings, those cheerful princes
Do not ask where they are
Their youth, those mornings
Those flesh-colored mists and showers
They are all gone, leaving not a trace
And yet, and yet
Where are the flowers of yesteryear?

Where are YOU? Where have you gone?
I'll go out to search
Who are you? Who, really?
Among whom have you been lost?
Among the crowd of lonely men who fill the town
When day's magnificent downfall dyes heaven and earth?
Among the men cramming the lighted trains hurrying through the
　　　underground network of labyrinths?
Among the men jerking off in a single row, in the spacious men's room
　　　of a terminal
Among the men shooting balls, ass to ass, in the perspective of a
　　　pachinko hall?
Among the men downing cups of sake, at a sake-storefront?
Among the braves marching zigzag, in helmets, with wood poles?
Among the warriors in Duralumin head-pieces and Duralumin shields?
Among the yakuza in *dabo* shirts? Among the tough guys with tattoos
　　　of Krikara the dragon king?
Among the young men at the festival wearing nothing but plain
　　　loincloths under short coats?
Chimney sweeps, plasterers, hard-hats
Killers, gangsters, bosses of the underworld
Blood-splattered slaughterers, blood-splattered fishmongers
A surgeon proud of his brawn, freshly, terrifically shaven

A singer with his bumptious throat, legs arched on the stage
Robber drivers of the dump trucks that speed in a string along night's
      highway
Pig iron handlers made of the same stuff as the iron burning in the blast
      furnace
Coal miners with their lighted heads, stark naked gold mine workers
Negro laborers in a diamond mine
The Minotaur in a dungeon, a centaur in a fury
A guardsman in a sealed bank who comes and goes like clockwork
      through the night
A diver who comes out of the heavy tide into light and painfully
      breathes
An oily-smelling crewman on the ocean route, sweaty-smelling
      fishermen off Las Palmas
A racing driver ablaze, at the moment of crashing to death into the car
      ahead
Boxers bathed in blood, hugging each other
Wrestlers mimicking love-making
Bank robbers, intelligence agents, guerrillas
Revolutionaries, stolidly silent communists
The Nazi Schutzstaffel, mounted policemen, soarers through the sky
      riding horses bareback
Ones who are on heaven's crossbeam, chest held high
Youths alive like stars
Young dead who have turned into stars in heaven

the MAN,	And you
again	Thinker astride a toilet, elbow on knee
	And chin rested on palm
	The thinking, powerful chin
	With the flesh thrusting up, cloven in two
	Lips tightly closed, knotted at the ends
	Deep philtrum, nose wings breathing like an accordion
	Dark nostrils, the hairs thriving in them
	Swollen eyelids, shadows cast by the lowered eyelashes
	Thick eyebrows pulled together, making a vertical
	groove like a deep scar
	And the weight on all these, the forehead
	Sorrow, sufferings, love, the whole of your history
	At the harsh top of you, thinking
	Smoldering in morning haze, your entire thought
	That is, your head, a globe
	Packed with your purple many-folded brain

Is equal in value to the other brains down under you, thinking
Responsible for procreation, many-folded, smoldering in evening haze
In the thorny shrub of gleaming wire and frizzy nettles
Equal to the gizzards of wisdom
Dangling ponderously, now exposed
For the briefs are slipped from the hairy thighs down to the knees
The ceaseless waves of joys and of sufferings
Which, rising from your hidden, sacred center
Cannot be caught by the naked eye
Make every muscle-path blaze fleetingly
Mounting onslaughts on both brains, above and below
Your gigantic, solitary image which is at the admirable center
Of all phenomena, all celestial bodies, all universes
Has, clinging to its stout neck
Its bulging shoulders, and its monolithic loins
All the pagan gods, all the holy spirits, and boys
You, who are at the venerable center of all
While seated on the toilet
Form the median point of the cross-shaped mysterious toilet floor
And the cross shape cut off with you, thinking
Goes under, creaking heavily
Into the dark earth, into the invisible red inside
You, who go under, who are power and are wisdom
You, who are gentleness, heaviness, and pureness
You, who are at the blazing center of all—who are you?
You, who are god of my gods, are NOWHERE
You on the cross-like toilet floor
Whom I have made up in my painful faith, are NO ONE
Ah!

Edward A Lacey

(1938 – 1995)

Edward Lacey left his native land shortly before the publication of his first book,
The Forms of Loss, *the first openly gay volume of poetry published in*
Canada. A wandering spirit, he spent many years in Latin America, North
Africa and Southeast Asia. Many of his poems reflect his life in Third World
countries, his social and erotic involvements with their people, and his political
commitment.

Ramon

Seven years ago, almost to the month and day.

It is not hard to pick a sailor up at Retiro Station.
They come in, hot and penniless, from the sex prison of their ships
        and the time prison of the sea,
ready to sleep anywhere, or do anything,
to the great city, grave city on the silver river
—the city that hides its loneliness in eating.
Even out of uniform, you can pick them out by their air of guilt and
        expectancy,
as they arrive in pairs at the plaza, eye the prospects, then separate,
loll on the grass, sprawl on benches, prowl the marble station,
circle the British clock tower, round and round, like a ship's deck,
with faintly rolling gait.
Conversation is easy. Sit down beside one on the park bench.
Ask him where he comes from, tell him you once passed through
        there on a train, offer him a cigarette, offer...
Brown country boys, desert sailors most of them, drafted and
        recruited
from Tucuman, Jujuy, Saltá, towns of the mestizo north,
they come to the park because they are sick of the sea and afraid of
        the city and Retiro at least reminds them of home,
as it vomits out all day the hopeful brown faces arriving from the
        country
to the dark city, sad city, cold city on the silver river.

Once you have picked one up, the search for a room:
the good hotels have fastidious doormen who look at you
      unnervingly;
the alojamientos have stereos and mirrors for men with women;
the hospedajes demand many documents and show you sex-
      perfumed cots in rooms for five.
Finally, success. Inside the room. Alone.
The touching of bodies. The bedding down. Lifebuoyed
clean smell of white-and-blue crinkly uniform, soon cast aside, then
      of firm young body
trembling cock already rampant, casting its shadow on the hard
      brown belly,
and a desire for human tenderness.

O all night in that boy's arms I lay after the tumbling,
as he slept with an erection, and in the morning did him again,
for the price of a pack of cigarettes and a hotel room.
Eighteen years old, from Mendoza, in the throes of sex and life.
He had been a naval cadet for just five months.
Soon he would sail away—in a week—for the Antarctic; he was
      afraid; he had never been there; was it really cold?
And did I want to meet him again Sunday night?
And as we rode back in the subway, returning to Retiro,
morning light hurting our eyes, ill-humoured city faces all around us,
      we filled with sleep and peacefulness,
the question, almost whispered: "Te gusté?" "Did you like me?"

Sunday night I got stupidly drunk, did not go to Retiro;
alcohol ruins the best moments of a manic-depressive, or perhaps
      instinctively
I didn't want to spoil it. Never saw him again.
Seven years ago that sailor set forth for Antarctica.

Mesón Brujo

The boy brought in the logs to start the fire.
A gust of night and nature blew in with him,
of animals out prowling in the dark.
His cheeks were bright with cold; his skin was white;
black hair hung low across a narrow forehead.

From my cold bed I watched him stack the logs
in a kind of pyramid, the small ones under,
the bigger ones on top, then saw him stick
chips of pitch pine among them, strike a match,
and light a sliver; and the room soon filled
with the resinous odour of *ocote* smoke.
Then he blew on the spark of fire he had created,
till the chips burned brightly, wrapping in their flame
the smaller logs, which in turn would ignite
the larger, to the largest one, on top.
And the room blossomed roses. All the while,
crouched at his task, he had not spoken, not looked at me,
but fixed his gaze on his logs with a concentrated
beetling frown, across which light and shadow played.
Now he got up, asked awkwardly if the fire
was satisfactory, and prepared to go.
And I answered yes, the fire was satisfactory
and no doubt would burn for at least two hours more,
time enough for me to fall asleep, while I thought
there was something much more satisfactory than fire
which would warm me even more. He left. I dozed.
Or perhaps I slept; the fact is, some hours later
—how many, I don't know—I heard, at least
it seemed I heard a sound, a hesitant tapping
at my door, and I rose in the fire's ambiguous light,
glided half-asleep over the hard, flat tiles,
opened the door effortlessly, as one does in dreams,
and the log-boy came in, cheeks bright red with cold.
There in the fire's dim glow I watched him undress,
saw the white body define itself from layers of dark clothing,
saw him stand, legs apart, in the rosy dying light,
black hair ingathering round an opening rose,
felt his icy skin, glabrous as myrtle bark,
as he slid into bed beside me. He was an expert
at lighting fires, but now it fell my turn
to stroke for the first time that cold virgin skin,
caressing rubbing it to raise a spark,
blowing on that spark to fan it to a flame,
wrapping him in my arms and legs to warm him,
playing each trick of friction, till at last,
like wood still green, he caught—The hard logs crumbled
to white ash; the last embers closed their eyes;
and in the darkness we were our own fire.

All night the log-boy tossed there in my arms
in intervals of sleep and waking dream,
all heat and flame now, in a bed as warm
as roses. Till I heard, just before morning,
another distant tapping at my door,
and the fire-boy noiselessly, as one does in dreams,
rose and in the white light of the false dawn
donned slowly his dark clothing, slid across
the smooth tiles to the door, opened it effortlessly
and was gone. And I lay asleep in the half-light.

The next night, after dinner, when the hour
for the guests to retire and the fires to be lit
arrived, I lay in bed, awaiting him,
but a gray-haired old man came to light my fire,
place the pine chips, build the log pyramid
in my cold chambers at the Mesón Brujo.

Rejean

On his chest he had tattooed "*vivre*,"
and I knew *just* what it meant
the night he sat down, uninvited,
at the table where I was drinking
in the dear, dead Altesse Tavern.
He spoke absolutely no English,
but we got along well enough.
Son of a poor farming family
from the country near Trois Rivieres,
he had come to the city,
like all boys, trying his luck.
His long black hair was lustrous.
His smile was young and mocking.
His cock was pale and urgent.
"Je suis aux hommes," he told me.

He stayed with me for one winter,
a season of discontent
(like all seasons in Canada),

and at night his pale candle consoled me
for my sun-skinned South Americans.
He cost me a lot of money,
for he liked to wear fine clothing;
he liked steak and seafood dinners;
he frequented PJ's nightclub,
where he joked with the transvestites
and drank *crème de cacao*
avec du lait (I paid,
but I got my *lait* for free).

He smoked a lot of dope,
and he dropped a lot of acid,
and he caused me all sorts of problems,
for all his friends were hoodlums
who belonged to *la petite pègre*.
He was basically a good boy,
but eighteen years old, and crazy.

He stayed with me all winter
and in the spring I left him,
because he cost me money,
and he caused me many problems,
and his feet stank most disgracefully,
and I grew tired of his penis
—as I grow tired of everything;
so in the end I left him
—as I leave everybody—
to go on with my searching.
And God knows what's become of him.

Rejean. His motto, *"vivre."*
And he lived for a while off me.

Poeme des Amours Fugitifs

Young Inca boy with a guitar:
the dark waterfall of your hair
splashed over me as we made love;
your body, slim and arched, above
me darted in and out
of my well-trained and willing mouth
until the salt sweet sperm came; then
at peace, accomplices and men,
we licked each other's sweaty skin,
confessed our prides and told our sins,
—a poet growing old, a young
confusion with a life-style—song—
and then sleep came and brought us dreams
of childhood, in each other's arms.

The gold of bodies does not melt;
preserves itself in what was felt.

Moroccan boys in mountain towns:
djellabas, snow-white or leaf-brown,
hid slim white cocks that like sharp knives
cut my ass; then the cool kif pipes;
Mexican boys, met on the road,
in jails, cantinas, briefly had
and disremembered; dusty faces,
small cocks, tight balls, great eagernesses;
Argentines, Uruguayans, complex
city boys needing simple sex;
treacherous, delicate Indian lads
from beautiful, deadly Trinidad;
—all of you are dimly with me yet;
I keep the faith; I do not forget.

The gold of bodies does not melt;
preserves itself in what was felt.

Brazilian boys with laughing cocks
earnest with need to get your rocks
off in some way, and set your seal
on woman, man or animal;

Dário, Fabrício, Adonai
—you will not age, you will not die;
my mind will keep you always young,
brown-skinned and eager and well-hung;
kisses you did not have to give,
and gave, I, while I live,
will recall, and how you would lie
beside me afterwards, till the sky
went white, and the bem-te-vi at dawn
woke us with his three-note song.

The gold of bodies does not melt;
preserves itself in what was felt.

This is not boasting, for who cares
these days? I have made love in cars,
especially taxis (always prefer
cabbies and shine-boys; they're quick and sure),
on beds and hillsides, in ruined churches,
on beaches, mountain-tops, under bridges;
and though I happen to dote on boys,
like Jews who've nothing against goys,
I hold no brief against the man
who lies with girl, sow, ewe, or ram;
and, growing older, only enthuse
for money, to keep on buying youths
to warm my age with their hot hands:
the best loves are one-night stands!

The gold of bodies does not melt;
preserves itself in what was felt.

Felice Picano

(1944 –

*Felice Picano is of the generation that emerged with Gay Liberation in the '70s
His pathbreaking 1980 anthology,* A True Likeness, *was the very first
collection of lesbian and gay writing. Best known for his novels and fictionalized
memoirs, Picano was part of the "Violet Quill Club" of New York gay writers
that also included Edmund White, Andrew Holleran and George Whitmore.
He was also involved in two important gay publishing ventures, the Sea Horse
Press, which he founded, and the Gay Presses of New York.*

The Deformity Lover

The first one he loved—an accident
was a deaf mute
golden lean as a West Coast
basketball star.
Surprised by his luck
all he could think of was sex.
Until after
when they spoke on sheets
writing messages in vaseline.
They met after that
once a week for some time.
The sex got hotter
their bodies fit better.
Then his speech began to slip.
Words seemed inexact
and harsh
compared to reading lips,
or making a point
with a fingertip
or a kiss.
Then the deaf mute went away.

The next one was a blind boy
at a college gym dance.
A curly head of hair
the body of a stevedore,

an Adriatic address,
convinced him this would be special.
He wasn't disappointed.
This time they talked
but softly,
never looking at each other
in the bedroom's blinded night:
letting touches rediscover
soft steppes of ribs,
meadows of flesh,
seas of infinite skin.
They got together often—
geographers of the tactile.
Each visit left him thinking
our senses—
so misused when there—
when missing, are seldom missed.
Then the blind boy found a lover.

Since then he's gotten bolder
searching
for what others pass over.
An afternoon with a veteran
who happened to have left an arm
in a rice-paddy in Viet Nam
disproves that two hands
are better than one.
A night with someone older
whose seizures
when he's ready to come
aren't orgasm, but pre-Grand Mal
becomes a game of sex
roulette.
Nothing indiscreet.
No ads in the papers for amputees.
No loitering near the handicapped
hoping a hunchback wants to connect.
It's beauty
not the grotesque he seeks.
But the only perfection he can see
is that most apparently,
poignantly
flawed.

This isn't a case from Kraft-Ebbing.
If asked,
he'd say he's a normal guy.
For him a chiselled profile is fine,
but handsomer with a speech defect.
A well-defined chest will evoke
his desire
but heavily scarred or mispigmented
its athletic cut is more gratifying.
Deformity is a grace, he'll say.
Like courage, it's clean
and always naive,
open and free, no hiding—
the truest state of man perhaps.
Want to see him use this philosophy?
You can find him almost every night
in any one of a half dozen bars.
He's a hospital ward
for the maimed young gods:
a port for anyone's surgical storm:
looking to fuck
the human condition.

Aches-les-Bains

Smoking, smashed on my cot
locked back in my room
after trashing an hour
through showers and saunas
I heard a guy croon
through the next-door partition
"I love you as much as God."

The whistle of sheets.
A flash slap on skin.
Another. Another. Another.
A tumult of stumbles.
One splintered gasp.
A moan. A thud—and then:
"More, I mean. More than God."

Straight Man

Cologne—like innocence that lasts too long
—wafts about his shoulders
This vanity of odor is surely someone wifely's purchase.
An inch of flesh beyond the athlete seemly
garlands at his buckle:
Insouciance of his figure is the man's estate
he's earned; he's learned to flaunt it.
You are certain now the tautness
in his trousers is available—and worth it.

A sense of suited comfort in his universe
where male is male and always first
Supports him through the annual round of crises.
Heir to ritual and position
He has given up ideals for calm and compromise
Let paychecks and martinis
tame the rebel-child adored by all, admired
In each mirror—transform him
into diaper-folder, bill-disburser, plumber.

Surprised by your attentions, shy, defenses
up, yet feeling proud he still attracts
(if only guys) he broadcasts by his stance
he may be open to indiscretion
If the come-on is original, the consequences nil.
He yawns, then straightens out his creases
Forgets about the roast at home
Those checkbook calculations two weeks late
Eccentric railroad schedules.

As still as prey in gunsight, he rises
to your challenge with inside debate you almost see:
Rage, disdain, dismissal are the obvious moves—
yet all too final. He wonders if an odd touch
Of adventure wouldn't add
a private glamour. It's years since he has dared
A dark and selfish deed. And so he smiles
at you—eighteen and horny once again....
And after sex, he always shows you
photos of the wife and kids.

Ian Young

(1945 –

Born in London, England, Ian Young was a pioneer gay activist in his adopted country, Canada. His early poetry coincided with the emergence of both Canadian literature and the Gay Liberation movement in the 1960s and '70s. A bibliographer, publisher and anthologist of gay literature, as well as a poet, he later chronicled the psychohistory of gay life and of the AIDS crisis. He lives in Toronto with Wulf, his partner of 15 years.

For Constantine Cavafy

Reading your book
I see you now
again in your Alexandria,
leaning
toward the window of a shop
where the light
catches the dust and touches
the features of a young man within. Watching,
you catch sight of your reflection
mottled in the glass,
and move away,
last words of a poem
rising to your mind:
      "Later, in a happier time,
      a man just like me
      will appear, and act freely."
Sometimes,
remembering my silences,
my lost moments,
the line of burnt-out candles,
I despair with you, Cavafy.
And then, sometimes,
I think: this is that happy time;
I am the man.

Standing and Kneeling Figures

his eyes are closed
parts of his nakedness glow
with the pleasure inflicted

his mouth is open
his face shines
with ecstasy and light

he is kneeling
leaning into darkness
his elbows pinned behind him
resemble wings

there is a slight pressure
from the gloved hand
above the head

without it he would faint
or levitate

the curve of his white back
glistens with dew

the black hand's mate
brushes where narrow wrists
nuzzle at steel boundaries

the earth
and the standing figure
anchor him

his mouth and hands are open
his eyes shine with nakedness
he would levitate
with ecstasy and light

a deep uneven breathing
as though an angel
trapped inside one lung
gasped for infinity

"take it slowly now"
the sound of keys
turning in silver locks

"take it slowly now
unfold your white wings
and fly"

Colossus of Rhodes

Colossus of Rhodes
standing astride the harbour
to honour the sun-god
(till the earthquake toppled it)—
less impressive than Chris
(a sun-god himself)
in his blue denim
standing astride nothing.

He
won't come to bed but
smiles his sly smile
as I unzip his fly,
kneel, and proceed to
blow my head off.

My colossus
is a little weak in the knees.
Yes,
one day, he'll topple too.

Honi Soit Qui May Y Pense

A boy of fifteen,
he wore a jacket, dark shirt, wool tie,
his bright eyes studying earnestly
Androcles and the Lion

in the Shavian alphabet...
His friend, a few years older,
blond and bundled in overcoat and scarf,
carried a flute
as they sat at the next table
of a café in Toronto.
My friend knew the younger boy
and I asked her who they were.
"He used to be a nice, ordinary kid,"
she said; "Then he met *him*—Brett.
Brett took him to Montreal,
did things to him... I don't know...
they're fags... you know... Music Room types."
When they left, they were laughing,
planning how to spend Brett's paycheck.
I noticed they'd written in Shavian
all over the serviettes.
That's what corruption does to you.

Home on the Range

"Oh! Cisco!"—Leo Carillo
"Oh! Pancho!"—Duncan Renaldo

Have you ever thought about how
those handsome young heroes in the western movies
so often have sidekicks to help them,
inseparable older companions, familiar yet
oddly deferential,
always taking the lead from the younger guy?
A curious relationship when you think of it.
What keeps the older man riding just a little behind
his lean young friend?
And why does our hero keep him around?
Sometimes the sidekick is stout and cantakerous
(in which case he would be played by Edgar Buchanan)
and sometimes long in the tooth and funny (Gabby Hayes).
Or he might be wise, stoical and a little sad (Ben Johnson).
Best of all, when the young traveller has no name

and looks like Clint Eastwood,
his older friend is quiet, tough and hot
and is Lee Van Cleef.
Once or twice Lee has saved Clint's life in a tight spot.
Even so, Lee figures he still owes Clint.
Owes him a lot.
So gunman and sidekick ride together and
face down the opposition (they're always outnumbered):
the sheriff and his posse, the bad guys, or the town.
Then they ride out when the job's done and
make camp for the night
cooking beans and bacon over an open fire,
crickets and the occasional wolf supplying the music.
They don't say much to each other, just a word or
two now and then, spitting into the fire.

Why do they ride together then, these two?
What strange hold does the young gunman have over his friend?
Does it ever occur to you
we never see these guys at home. Do they have a home?
Actually they do:
a comfortable ranch-house
with some ground around it for cattle,
dogs and now and then a young trail-hand or two
brought in to help with the chores and provide some
company.
So let's look in on them.
We'll say it's Clint and Lee this time,
just to be sexy about it.
Lee's a dangerous man but Clint
knows how to handle him and
has Lee haul in more wood while
Clint lounges in the big chair in front of the log fire,
one leg slung over the chair arm. He's
cleaning his gun and
watching his friend sweat.
He's half asleep but keen as a coyote,
a little smile playing on his lips.
He snaps his fingers and Lee
drops to his knees and
nuzzles Clint's swelling blue-jeaned crotch.
Clint takes his time rolling a cigarette.
Lee lights it, striking the match with one hand.

Clint offers him the first puff. The rest is Clint's as
Lee, on his knees, has other things to do with his face.
Clint's strong hand ruffles the balding head between his legs
and a brass fly-button
pops out of its slit.
He takes off his belt, runs it
through his hands like a fresh-shot rattler and
cracks it, suddenly, like a lariat.
Lee hisses and feels Clint's boot on his neck. It creaks.
The fire is hot on his back and rear. The saddle
lying on the buffalo rug
shines in the orange flame-light.
It'll be a long, cold night outside,
but warm in here, for them.
"I want it, boss," Lee whispers.
The tobacco-stained hand, one finger-joint missing,
gently strokes the young gunman's thigh.
"Earn it then."
(His eyes narrow to slits; his teeth clench.)
"Earn your pay." (The pay packet
seems to be growing as Lee fondles it,
thinking about a bonus.)

In the bunkhouse, the new hired hands,
real goodlooking, both of them, but just boys,
have stripped to their longjohns and are fooling around
tying each other up with rawhide by the light of an oil lamp,
thinking about Clint and Lee.

Sex Magick

My boyfriend is a magician.
Once when I came home unexpected,
I saw him leaning forward, hands on his knees,
talking in growls, whispers and low mutterings
to a little man made of smoke,
odd-shaped like a cloaked dwarf,
dark and hovering in the air,
made of the air but looking like a thing of ink
at the bottom of the sea.

As I opened the apartment door, the being
twisted suddenly like a cape
caught by a gust of wind and
dissolved, filling the apartment
with grey smoke and a
lingering smell,
burnt, but delicate, like scorched jasmine or
lavender.
"Stove acting up again?" I remarked,
sniffing and hanging up my coat.

My boyfriend is an enchanter.
The day I met him I
stopped in my tracks,
forgot the day's errands and important meeting and
turned back
only to encounter him.
Yet I had not seen him.
It was when, magick book in hand, he
peered through a bush at me
like Priapus piping in the Arcadian trees
I knew he wanted me.
I didn't know for what.

My boyfriend is a high priest.
Robes hang in my bathroom. Wands
lean in the hall, incense burning in brass.
The basement walls are covered with jars holding
powders, herbs, salts, dried things.
It was his spell
brought us to this house, so
it's only right I juggle words and numbers
to keep it. Were we to leave,
the landlord would be puzzled
at the strange circles painted on his floor,
runes marked on the wainscotting,
talismans over the door.
Our landlord would try to examine them
(to find out how to remove them of course).
He would spend a great deal of time over the problem.
He would become more and more absorbed.
His wife would begin to worry
about his state of mind lately.

Slowly, the markings would begin to take shape for him,
would alter him. And then...
But our landlord and his wife are definitely
not ready for this.
So of course we stay,
and make ourselves at home,
with their co-operation.

My boyfriend is a shaman.
When his black cat died, his familiar,
something went out of our relationship.
I can't replace Pootz but have tried
to take his place
and my boyfriend, I think,
knows this and
works magick through me.
Because of it and out of
deference to my wishes, he
refrains from filling our house with snakes,
weasels and other small creatures.
Instead, there are stuffed bears,
teddy bears in his bedroom,
library and on the stair.
Hello Providence (head wedged between the bannisters).
Ah! Mephistopheles, face down in the towel pile.
All his bears have names.

My boyfriend is a conjurer.
Sometimes I feel myself more
like a winged horse than a man
when he wants to ride me.
And sometimes he just makes me disappear
in a traditional puff of smoke
for a few moments or
a few months at a time.
When he brings me back,
a little dazed but
more or less ready for action, I always find
the joints he's rolled for me on the mantle,
just behind that blank, gazing white Egyptian head.

My boyfriend seems to be a yogi.
One Saturday morning when I was elsewhere,

he phoned (how did he know where I was?)
and asked if I was coming home and
would I bring (as usual) his *TV Guide*
to see what old movies are in store for us this week.
When I arrived we got cozy in the sunroom and he
unbuttoned his jeans and presented
his cock to me, impaled
with a needle he'd
run through the skin beneath the cock-head and
replaced with a golden ring.
There was no swelling and
only the merest speck of blood,
powdery and dry like a spot of rust.
He soon had me leashing his cock like a falcon
at my hand till he spilled in it;
and all that night he worked sex magick through me.
People came up to me in the street,
I was proposed to by women and men,
boys looking for their first adventure
would find *me.*
And my hand on the jacketed back of a student
burned, he said, like a hot iron.
My boyfriend had made me literally hot,
body temperature at fever point yet
I had no fever...
When I walked into a bar the first person I saw
was a quiet young man from the same
English suburb I grew up in.
He came home with me and was transformed
into a living incarnation of the wolf-god,
eyes flashing and hooded, growls
deep in the throat, rain-damp
fur standing on end,
and in the black focus of his eyes as they
commanded me,
the image of a young Pan,
trampling the erect earth in antic joy.

My boyfriend is a sorcerer
and in our garden there is a circle of painted stones.
Once, at night, I thought I saw
tiny figures
holding some miniature rite

under their darkness.
But when we are there,
my boyfriend's white blouse and trousers
catch the moonlight in a way I cannot forget.
And I am Pegasus again,
his name for me.

My boyfriend is a man of impulse.
His hands alter the weather
(he can rearrange small clouds like chess-pieces);
he travels at will. In his need
he can wound me
but only once has failed to match his word to me.
He was with another man and I was in Central Park,
worrying. A sudden storm,
hail, lightning and hurricane wind
smashed through the park,
levelling trees and
turning the paths to rivers
and the monument steps to waterfalls.
My back, hit by a falling bough
sheared from a huge oak tree
was bruised black and cut, my hands
scraped and raw, my neck ripped.
Others were sure my boyfriend had tried to kill me.
I knew otherwise. It was the gods
warning him
of his power over me,
of how easily he could hurt me.

My boyfriend is a philosopher
when he is with me
of a morning in the sunroom,
listening to music, smoking dope and planning...
There I am his amanuensis and
make marks on a paper as he speaks to me.
Sometimes I don't understand what I write—
runes on a cryptic wall—
but I type them up, the letters
jumping about and
changing places with one another
until they are his and mine,
the way he wants it.

And when he is not in our house
and I am here alone to water the cats and
feed the plants and inhabit,
when he is not here,
when I wait for him
the house is always in shade.
There are few sounds.
My typewriter seizes up.
The record player utters only a tiny tinny voice,
essential things disappear until he returns
and there is a cold chill
in certain areas of the basement.
A creak on the stair,
a tap-tapping in the pantry, but
no-one is there.
Only I am there, left
with these papers, these words.
Left alone
in a house of bears.

Sex Magick (Epilog)

My boyfriend is a sorcerer.
First time I spoke to him he
held the Golden Dawn in his hand.

And
in my dream the sword
so heavy
only courage could raise.
Sliced precisely in half
I awoke suddenly
whole.
Trembling.
Sweating.
Full of fears.

One foot in the grave.
One foot on the path.

Antler

(1946 –

Author of many books and recipient of numerous awards, his book-length
poem, Factory, *won him plaudits from many of the great poets of our day.*
Antler's poems of ecology and Eros-ology have appeared worldwide.
He continues to live in the city of his birth, Milwaukee, and tries to spend at
least a month in the wilderness each spring and each fall.

What Every Boy Knows

Every boy knows what it's like
    when he's really alone,
When it's safe to jack off with a passion,
When it's safe to take off his clothes
    and prance around
And parade his lubricating cock
    before every mirror in the house,
Safe to cry out and talk dirty
    while jerking it,
Really scream "I'm coming!"
    when he comes,
Really stand on his head
    and jack off in his face
    if he wants,
Yes, every boy knows
    when it's safe.

At the country picnic the 12 year old boy
    wanders off by himself in the woods,
    he knows the perfect spot,
On his study-hall break to the library
    the 13 year old stops in the empty john,
    just enough time for a quickie,
The 14 year old boyscout waits till he's sure
    everyone in the tent is sleeping,
    quietly, slowly he plays with his dream,

The 15 year old boy runs home from school,
    half-way he's already hard,
His heart is pounding
    when he opens the frontdoor,
He knows he's got a full hour
    before his sister or parents return,
Enough time to give himself
    a real workout in the bathtub,
The 16 year old wakes up in the snowy night,
    he watches himself with a flashlight
    magically masturbate under the comforter,
The 17 year old puts *Leaves of Grass* aside,
    leans back on the chair with his feet on the wall
    in the basement at home where he studies,
He likes poetry, but right now
    he needs a really good handjob
    before he can continue...
No one can see me now, the boy chuckles to himself,
And I'm not fool enough anymore to think God
    is watching me horrified
    and will sentence me to hell.
If God doesn't love to watch boys jack off
    as much as boys love to watch themselves jack off
    he does not exist.
The 18 year old boy licks his lips
    as he jacks off in the hayloft,
If anyone saw me they'd think I was nuts
    he thinks as he squirms and groans,
His devilish lasciviousness to make love to himself
    makes the monkeys at the zoo seem prudes.
There's no posture, no expression on his face,
    no possible method of touch he won't try
    to make it feel more Wow.
The voluptuous 19 year old youth knows
    he's got the whole beach to himself today,
He basks naked in the sun till baked,
    then floating on the bosom of the lake
    gives himself the best handjob of his life.
The 20 year old mountainclimber still likes to masturbate
    when he's on top of a mountain alone,
He never tells anyone about it, it's a secret
    he keeps to himself,

He still smiles remembering the first time
        he jacked off from a cliff,
The ecstatic boyhood semen spurting and spurting,
        tumbling thousands of feet
        into the wild valley below...

Hot Summernight Cloudburst Rendezvous

The two boys embracing in the thunderstorm
Don't care if they get drenched,
Don't care if as they strip each other
        their clothes drop in lightninglight
                into puddles
        and are kicked laughingly into the mud.
It's the first time they've kissed each other,
The first time either of them ever kissed
        a boy
And neither has ever kissed
        a girl
And neither ever kissed before
        with his tongue.
They had no idea
        how passionate
                passion could be—
        they can hardly believe it,
That merely putting their lips together
        could be so...
                ah.
For a moment they stand apart
        silently gazing at each other
                in the flashes and thunder,
Centuries of Boyhood, Aeons of BoyLove
        proud in their playful smiles,
Knowing just what they're going to do,
        even though they never did it before,
Knowing that before long
        each of them is going to jack off
                the first boy they ever jacked off
        besides themself,

Knowing both of them can come
      and giving in, giving themselves
      to boyfriendship's ultimate gesture,
Knowing they both know
      how to jack off real good
      and aren't going to stop frenching
          while they whimper toward the brink.
Sure, it's beautiful
      to see a boy you love
          ejaculate in the lightning in the rain,
Crying with pleasure while the thunder thunders
      and the sky ejaculates millions of raindrops
As you squirm in rapture
      on the muddy grass
          under the tossing trees.

Shying Away

Seeing a boy go in a bookstore
I go in to get a closer look.
One glimpse is all I can stand.
The love of beautiful boys
Is as beautiful as beautiful boys.
Just looking for two seconds
Too much for me.
I feel faint, breathless,
Dazed as I rush back out
Plunging into the crowd.
Yet the air smells of spring.
I see flowers blooming.
I realize I am still
A creature of the woods.
A wild animal untamed.
Yet I think a beautiful boy
Might coax me
With gentle talking
And a soft song
To come closer,
To eat from his hand.

On My Way to Lake Michigan Sunrise
On the Milwaukee Lakefront Breakwater

In spring a smell comes from the Earth,
      my nostrils widen,
And I find myself staying up all night walking,
Remembering how many nights I've stayed up all night
      walking,
Thinking of all the boys asleep
      in beds in the dark houses
      in the sleeping neighborhoods
        surrounding me,
Picturing all the sleeping boys as I pass,
      their postures, expressions, movements,
Wondering which houses walked by
      hold what possibilities
      of warm and carefree young friends,
So close from this sidewalk, behind what doors,
      up what stairs, into which rooms,
      on what beds,
Sleeping boys with erections
      and the postures, expressions, movements
      of sleeping boys with erections
        they never know they have—
I stop, stand motionless for a minute,
      struck by the thought,
Looking up at the stars
      to honor them.
The whole city sleeps,
Not even a solitary car,
The first birds sing in the twilight.
All the erections boys have in their sleep
      and never know they have
      I know they have, I feel.
One man in the blue-dark smell of spring
      walking toward sunrise Lake Michigan,
Honoring the boys in the dark sleeping
      with erections they'll never know they had.

For Blowjob Power

For all their fast-talk and macho,
For all their postured coldness
        and manner of superiority,
Rowdy, tough, joking,
Wary or contemptuous,
Once naked, once spreadeagled
        on the silk bed
It's a different story.
Now silent, deep-breathing,
        motionless,
Completely given to the experience
        of homosexual joy,
Completely lost in total abandon
        to the swirling tongue,
        to the sucking mouth
As the boyloving lover
        performs his love
Feasting not only on the cock
        and balls,
But the whole crotch,
Service divine,
        delicately done,
Yet fierce with devotion,
        with worship.

Yes, how many boys so boisterous
        and punky before,
Are reduced to silent naked forms
        gazing at the
        passionate ravishing
        blowjob mouth
        with awe
Finding it hard to believe
        anything could feel so good.
How many boyhoods distilled
        into the unquestionable essence
        of a whimpered sigh,
The look of absolute ecstasy
        on their face,
Tamed and made gentle again
        by the blowjob mouth.

The Immortality of Boylove

It does no good to make boylove illegal
Or to believe it's a sin punished by hell,
To imagine it's a rare mental illness
            or to pretend it doesn't exist.
Boylove is everywhere.
As long as there are boys
            there will be the love of boys.
Millions of boys understand this.
They know what boylove is
            every time they jack off.
If you want to get rid of boylove
Assassinating me won't solve your problem.
Boys do not love boys
            only because they read my poems.
And if they did, it would be
            no less beautiful.
Burn all my poems if you want,
            it won't do any good.
As sure as the violet comes up every May
            on every continent on earth
            boylove continually unfolds.
The only way to destroy boylove on earth
            is to destroy the world.
And even if you did
            there are a billion suns in our galaxy
            and a billion galaxies
            in the visible universe!
More planets with BoyLove Utopias exist
            than all the boylovers or boys
            that've ever existed on earth!
Every time you denounce homosexuality
            10,000 beautiful boys
            ejaculate in their bestfriend's mouth!

William Barber

(1946 – 1994)

*William Barber was born and raised near Longfellow's Wayside Inn, just
outside of Boston. At the age of 19 he moved west to attend San Francisco
State, from whence, influenced by the city's growing hippie and arts scene, he
began publishing numerous poems, stories, and a successful series of comic
porno novels (as Billy Farout). He died of AIDS.*

The Gay Poet

I have broken the sound barrier of morality
with one crunchy bite on the phallic biscuit.
In my boyish womanhood, with my soul in drag,
I have been personal concubine to hundreds
of queens and princes, mistress of many
hedonists, lover of all.

I have pricked, prodded, pampered and pumped,
held my knees to my ears in the amyl twilight
and gone totally and obtusely mad, because
one halfway beautiful man weighed
a thousand tons on my fragile psyche.
My anima is stripped by the sight of my
wrinkled ego hanging out his back pocket
always two steps ahead of me.

I will go on, unknown lovers in my future,
I will be there, waiting with my mouth in my hand
to show you the ways into my body / being,
curling my wits to help you laugh out your orgasms,
but I am totally insane
because one of you, one too many of you
walked out that morning with all my reason
crumpled inside your tawny levis.

A Fuck Poem in the Tradition of Reality
for Gerry Fabian

"A man who will wear white mukluks will do anything!"—Bradley

Yes he was gorgeous and danced like a hot bull
hauling through town. In the black-walled bar
that swings like Rio, yes the dancehall,
the baboon's favorite tree, Fabian,
(because you wanted to know what happened)
I was out of cigarettes and in love.

Yes he took me to his house that was a tent
with a painted parachute ceiling
and muslin circular walls, saying:
"I have a carton of Camels. I'll give you a pack
to smoke before and after on the mattresses."
A sheik, or chic, or cheeks, a moving statue's body.
I gave him my legs and arms like clay mallets
and our backs and asses twisted all night
long.

So when I woke in the morning and lay still an hour
watching his sleeping, I gradually talked myself
out of that wish to stay there, repeating it.
I've learned the grapes, how each morning
is a new morning, how surfaces heal. The only thing
he saw me take with me was the Camels.
I smoked them for a day, to cover the empty spaces.

Yet this week when I saw him again, outside the bar
someone else was admiring his mukluks.
I was in a doorway dodging the rain, they didn't see me
as they crossed in front of me. But I heard
a slice of dialogue that was the real fucking.
I heard the bull boy say to the new face:
"I have a carton of Camels. I'll give you a pack."

Hustler Joe

Joe is going back to Arkansas, says it's "on account" his
Dad's sick and his brother has a job building boats and
drives a Cougar. At the hotel, Joe paid his bill by sell-
ing sections of his pink flesh to San Francisco on the wide
meat highway. Said it was a pain in the ass. "Course,
so's the war" he said, preferring women. Yet old Joe really
gave a man his money's worth; he'd roll either way, fag
fucking, nothing to it but a little hurting, nothing to a
mouthful of hot jizz, even an old man's jizz, so long's he's paying.

We was buddies, me and Joe. I'd screw him before he'd go
out, just to get him loose, for his consumers. At night,
sometimes, he'd blow me if the lights were out. Such a
pretty face, real blond hair, marine cut, the "shits" and
"jesuses" completely natural. Ten dollars hid in the bible,
six in his pocket, on the prowl. Joe walked through rain
like it wasn't raining, looked at a green wall and a torn shade
and saw only his thoughts, beer, broads, the open road.

Tomorrow morning he'll take the greyhound to Fayetteville,
the Ozark mountains. They said $44.25 for a one way ticket.
I gave him ten dollars for a ride on his back, dreaming of
horses on the green slopes of Appalachia, but he was still
$25.00 short. He pulled up his pants and we said goodbye
forever I guess, and he was back on the street in his blue
snugs with his big smile, so available. If interested,
please write to this poem, care of the wind, because by now
Joe's been gone so long he's fathered his own kids in Arkansas.

Explanation

I am not gay by your definition.
I will not stand in the drab beige men's room
like a fern watered with urine,
and wait for penises. I'm sorry.
Morality will just have to change.

I speak directly to the sons of
your officials, under the moon,
with the professors listening.

We have burned the closet door in effigy.
There will be no more watching for the feet
of policemen under the partitions.
                           Nor
the mediocrity of masses of shuffling gays
in the dark bars, ghettoed and ethnic.

I love men. I tell them so directly.
Wherever we encounter, there are no categories.

Michael Lassell

(1947 –

*Michael Lassell, the author of six books, is an editor by trade and a writer by
inclination. He says he writes poems because he has to, stories because he wants
to, essays because people ask him to, and travel articles because he enjoys getting
away from New York City as often as possible. He lives in Greenwich Village
and thinks Chelsea Boys and people who smoke cigars should all be killed.*

Times Square Poems

1.
Gino

This morning I clipped my nails,
in case I ran into Gino again.
Gino's a stripper at the
Gaiety Burlesk on 46th off
Broadway, the last of six dancers
five times daily and
well worth the wait.

There's only one way to
run into Gino
and it isn't by chance:
pay your six bucks at the door—
five if you've got a coupon from
The Village Voice—then
poke around in the dark with
the other fat fruits until
the lights come up and
decorum goes down like
the *Titanic.*

Last night,
in the small room
behind the stage,
he brought me off for

25 bucks as
one finger of my
right hand
wormed into
his asshole.

I carried the smell of him
home with me—
talc, sweat, and fear. I mean,
hygiene has its place, but
I let him linger. I
wasn't about to
wash him off as if
he'd never been there.
I owed him more than
the canned scent
housewives use to
freshen up
their porcelain.

2.
The going rate

The going rate is
40 bucks but
some of them will
do it for less weekdays.
Alberto did it for
30 because I was
"nice."

Tony said he'd go with me
for 20 but
Tony's got a dollar sign
cut into the hair at the
back of his head, and
Tony is not
Alberto, though
it was sweet of him
to offer.

In the back room
Alberto slips off his

clothes, then
mine. There is no
kissing, of course,
nothing that might
leave a mark on his
pride. Alberto's straight,
you see, or so he says.
Still, he's more direct
than most people you'll encounter
on a Thursday.

I come fast and apologize:
my semen gets
on his shoe.
"Part of the work," he says
with an accented grin and
wipes it off, then me.

If you want to
get off with Alberto
bring cash
and believe when he says
"I like you" that he's
never said it before
and won't again
before sunrise.

3.
Stud

His name is Jason; he's
"Italian" and "twenty."
Actually, Jason is the name of
whoever is dancing third
because that's what
the sign says out front
(these boys do have
a following).
He starts his second dance with
a hard-on that
softens in the
shuffle for
attention, but

it's never lost
for long.

Jason has a
lot of admirers.
Also a wife and child in
Puerto Rico.
Between shows—after a
"private performance" that
leaves him sapped
and sweaty as
a cane cutter—
he tries to call
San Juan on
the pay phone to see if
they came through
the hurricane
unscathed.

Of course, the phones
are out, lines
down, signals
dead.

He has the eyes of a Virgin and
pecs like the gifts of the Magi:
gold for wealth because he is
king of the roost;
frankincense because he is
the high priest of the
low in heart;
myrrh for cunning
because it heals my soul
just to look at him
and to know that
as long as there's money
there's a hairy chest
for my hand
somewhere in the world—
and I'll never go hungry
again.

4.
How to find love in an instant

Sit as close to the stage as possible.
Look like you're one of the kind who's buying and
like you've got the wherewithal.
Look into his eyes.
Look into his lap.
Covet him as loud as you can without speaking.
Do not touch. Just worship silently.

Applaud; show
appreciation. At the end of the set
let him approach you in the lounge where
Boys Meet Boys. He will put
one hand on your left tit and one on the
tight bundle of your jeans and
offer a private session for 40 bucks.
If you've got it, give it.
Don't dicker.

After you're both naked, he'll
rub his oiled body against yours.
You will be hard and hot and
grateful. He will be soft and bored
but attentive.

You will walk out into the night and no longer be
afraid of 42nd Street.
Now you are a part of it
and the locals can tell.
You will smile to have been accepted
and descend the subway stairs
knowing yourself better than ever
and better than ever
thinking yourself just fine.

Daddy

Oh, Daddy,
I'm far away and miss you
so much. The bogeyman is on the
prowl again, draped in last year's
judgment. Things go bump
in the cold sweaty night,
growl in the swelling neck and
sunken groin where men have danced
on points of pins
and Sabu rode his elephant
all the morning long in rain.

Kiss me quiet in the
moonless room. Tell me about
Heaven and how good boys turn to angels
when they die;
how you'll be there to meet me—
like that dream of disembarking
in the Land of Dead and
Grandpa's Airedale Mickey
lumbered up to lick my hand—
how you played hooky from school and
snuck off to Broadway to
steal a piece of Fanny Brice;
and how God loved his only son
so much He killed him.

Remember the time we went to
Radio City and saw
Ben-Hur from the first and only
row? You ate popcorn and were
Charlton Heston with
your arm around my chair,
your shoulder straining on the
reins. I was happy as Haya
Harareet to ride your chariot
anywhere.

I dreamed once I was crucified
but felt nothing, was shot
as many times as St. Sebastian

but did not complain, was
hoisted by a hook around my
breastbone—eyes skyward like
a saint or martyr—but
it did not hurt. That's how
pain is in dreams: all concave
terror, but pain in life is
terror and agony too. No wonder
passion can have two meanings.

And God whispered:
This is my beloved son in whom I am well pleased.
And Jesus was so moved
he gladly gave his life
for a stranger.

Oh, Daddy,
all I ever wanted was to
crawl into your arms, as firm
as hairless Samson's buttock cheeks.
Naked and enslaved, he grunts the
prison treadmill round, trapezius muscles
rising to the task. You bought me that
beefcake Bible for my confirmation,
and it more or less confirmed
what you feared.
I was grateful for Samson's he-man flesh, for
Jesus' long untangled hair
and angels gentle as
bathing or Hedy Lamarr.

Oh, Daddy,
wherever you are, I still want to
suck your chest hair, sink
into your skin like the
painless dream lashings of
a leather scourge, spread
tattoos across your stung trunk
like oil from Hedy's cruet
rubbed into the sore and
musk Semitic meat of Victor Mature as
John the Baptist—no!
that's not right (that was Rita

Hayworth dropping veils)—
as *Samson,* rather, pulling down
the temple by its columns,
loincloth stiff on glistening limbs
anointed by angry desire.

Secrets spill in the dark aisles
of theaters and churches
like blood from test tubes spreading
contagion. All I wanted was to
touch your cock that time
in the shower once when
I was small. Shame feels like
déjà-vu these days, but still
I love a shower room full of
nude men dripping water through
marble swirls of hair.

Oh, Daddy,
it was you all the time in those
back-room bars and bathhouse crannies
at four a.m.,
all those men who
filled me with the
Holy Spirit. I was
speaking in tongues. And when the
profane angel death comes
flapping down with winks and
wings akimbo, I will
recognize his sultry and
engendering breath, will
look into his bedroom eyes,
and see you there:
the dusky idol of my
'50s matinee,
strong and silent,
sullen as Gregory Peck's
lower lip lusting after
Bathsheba in a Technicolor dream.

How to be a Hedonist
for Gavin Dillard

Know that it isn't easy.
Give yourself permission
to fail. Most do. It is no
disgrace. Many begin by
finding a lover to
lose themselves in, a body that quivers as
bodies should and
deeper than you've ever
imagined. If you cannot live
for pleasure, live for love or
for the moment. Trace the curves of your
lover's back with cool lips and
hot intentions. Failing that,
live whatever way you can.
Nobody is perfect. Nobody is
keeping track.

Little you have learned will aid you.
"All good things must come to an end"
is *not* a hedonist credo. Neither is:
"A stitch in time saves nine."
Neither is:
"A penny saved is a penny earned."
Generally speaking, if
your mother learned a thing from
her mother, it will not
help you.
It is better to say:
"I'd give up everything for you,"
but it is not best
to believe it.

Reading is irrelevant.
What you need to know is not
in books. You must learn from
trial and error. If you must read books,
do not read anything written by an American
prior to *Tropic of Cancer.*
Do not read poetry by T.S. Eliot or by
Ezra Pound. Do not read

Dante or Goethe or
anything by a Scandinavian, a Lutheran, or
a computer programmer.
Do not read Greek tragedy unless
you think it's funnier than
Roman comedy. Read instead the moods
of your lover's eyes. Try to
outguess them.

Do not think.
No matter what.
No matter how much you are moved or
tempted to do so. Unless you are one of the few—
one of the rare few—for whom ideas
are sensual, for whom
concepts slide like heavy cream
around the white porcelain bowl of your brain,
unless abstractions
tickle the inside of your thighs
like a ride downhill taken
as a child. If you must think,
invent new ways to make love
without accoutrements.

If you must think, in spite of all advice
to the contrary, if you must think of
other things than love,
do not
express your thoughts. Thoughts given tongue
can kill. There is no
antidote for an aphrodisiac
more effective than a thought
spoken aloud.

If you must think your thoughts aloud
speak softly and
in metaphor.
Do not say:
"The trade embargo imposed against the
legitimate government of Nicaragua by the
right-wing faction of the Republican Party
causes me as much anxiety as the threat of
nuclear annihilation."

Say, rather:
"The flavor of your skin
gives me reason to live."

No matter what happens, do not
despair. Five senses are not many,
but they are sufficient. One alone is
sufficient if
properly handled. Start
with one. Practice. Become
a gourmet. An aficionado. A
connoisseur. When you have
mastered one, try another. Try them
in concert.
It is not impossible to enjoy all five senses
at once, but it is impudent and
inadvisable. Indulging more than three senses
at any one time is
superfluous. Any fool can see that,
even an old fool with
new tricks.

Do not live in a cold place.
Do not live under martial law
or inhabit any nation ruled by
a zealot.
Do not live in a country at war with
itself or in any territory occupied by
the Soviet Union, and do not dwell in
Israel, Jordan, or Lebanon—even if you are
a journalist (and it is not wise to be
a journalist: fact is anathema to hedonism).
There are lamentably few places left
to live. Do not live
in most of the United States. Do not live
near a factory or a retirement
village. Try to live in a Catholic country,
but do not live in the vicinity
of a church, unless it is very old and beautiful
and named for a saint with a past.

Live on a tree-lined street in a city with
parks, views, broad boulevards, and

excellent native cuisine.
Live there a long time in love until you take
everything for granted.
Then move, leaving your lover behind because
his skin is beginning to taste
salty.

Take up an occupation that requires little
regimen. Move to a small apartment
by yourself. Drink large quantities of
alcoholic beverages. Lose control. Speak to
strangers in strange bars. Follow them home
by taxi or on foot whether or not you're
invited. Taste their skin.
Lie to them.
Lie to yourself. Dream.
Forget your dreams. Live
for the moment. Think that
the scent on the spring air reminds you of
someone you left behind.

Turn suddenly, without warning, in public at a
voice like his voice. Eat. Drink. Be merry,
for tomorrow you die, and the next day too.
Receive a telegram.
Follow its directions to a graveyard.
Do not ask questions. Ever.
Read the inscription on the headstone.
Say the name aloud without
moving your lips. Listen to
the granite. Touch it with
your tongue. Smell the dead
flowers. Say:
"The taste of your skin
gives me reason to live."
See if you mean it.
Leave in tears.
Develop an irrational appetite for
salt.
Have neurotic dreams. Remember your
dreams.

How to Watch Your Brother Die

When the call comes, be calm.
Say to your wife, "My brother is dying. I have to fly
to California."
Try not to be shocked that he already looks like
a cadaver.
Say to the young man sitting by your brother's side,
"I'm his brother."
Try not to be shocked when the young man says,
"I'm his lover. Thanks for coming."

Listen to the doctor with a steel face on.
Sign the necessary forms.
Tell the doctor you will take care of everything.
Wonder why doctors are so remote.

Watch the lover's eyes as they stare into
your brother's eyes as they stare into
space.
Wonder what they see there.
Remember the time he was jealous and
opened your eyebrow with a sharp stick.
Forgive him out loud
even if he can't
understand you.
Realize the scar will be
all that's left of him.

Over coffee in the hospital cafeteria
say to the lover, "You're an extremely good-looking
young man."
Hear him say,
"I never thought I was good enough looking to
deserve your brother."

Watch the tears well up in his eyes. Say,
"I'm sorry. I don't know what it means to be
the lover of another man."
Hear him say,
"It's just like a wife, only the commitment is
deeper because the odds against you are so much
greater."

Say nothing, but
take his hand like a brother's.

Drive to Mexico for unproven drugs that might
help him live longer.
Explain what they are to the border guard.
Fill with rage when he informs you,
"You can't bring those across."

Begin to grow loud.
Feel the lover's hand on your arm
restraining you. See in the guard's eye
how much a man can hate another man.
Say to the lover, "How can you stand it?"
Hear him say, "You get used to it."
Think of one of your children getting used to
another man's hatred.

Call your wife on the telephone. Tell her,
"He hasn't much time.
I'll be home soon." Before you hang up say,
"How could anyone's commitment be deeper than
a husband and wife?" Hear her say,
"Please. I don't want to know all the details."

When he slips into an irrevocable coma,
hold his lover in your arms while he sobs,
no longer strong. Wonder how much longer
you will be able to be strong.
Feel how it feels to hold a man in your arms
whose arms are used to holding men.
Offer God anything to bring your brother back.
Know you have nothing God could possibly want.
Curse God, but do not
abandon Him.

Stare at the face of the funeral director
when he tells you he will not
embalm the body for fear of
contamination. Let him see in your eyes
how much a man can hate another man.

Stand beside a casket covered in flowers,
white flowers. Say,
"Thank you for coming," to each of several hundred men
who file past in tears, some of them
holding hands. Know that your brother's life
was not what you imagined. Overhear two
mourners say, "I wonder who'll be next?" and
"I don't care anymore,
as long as it isn't you."

Arrange to take an early flight home.
His lover will drive you to the airport.
When your flight is announced say,
awkwardly, "If I can do anything, please
let me know." Do not flinch when he says,
"Forgive yourself for not wanting to know him
after he told you. He did."
Stop and let it soak in. Say,
"He forgave me, or he knew himself?"
"Both," the lover will say, not knowing what else
to do. Hold him like a brother while he
kisses you on the cheek. Think that
you haven't been kissed by a man since
your father died. Think,
"This is no moment not to be strong."

Fly first class and drink Scotch. Stroke
your split eyebrow with a finger and
think of your brother alive. Smile
at the memory and think
how your children will feel in your arms,
warm and friendly and without challenge.

Dancer(s) with Dick(s)
at the 1 Saloon, Key West

I have one hand on his cock, the other
deeply involved with the shaven everything between his balls and asshole, at which

willing target I've aimed my spit-slick thumb.
"All *right,*" he says, bending to help me and
offer a kiss, "work *me!*" I don't want to

disappoint, so I pop one proffered tit
in my mouth while he grinds that totally
tubular rod of his into my palm.

"My name is Chris," he says. He's a solo
tonight (the other dancer's father had
a stroke). "You *are* a hot daddy," he says,

which takes me aback (I feel twenty-six
most of the time). I give him another
buck: "I guess I'm getting there," I shuffle.

"No getting there involved," he says, his brown
forehead a furrow, "you have *arrived.*" I
take him at his word—after all, he's the

pro. He might just be right. So, now I'm a
daddy, I think and let it sink slowly
in. Well, it's better than nothing, I guess—

here at the far end of further away
than anywhere and way beyond what the
hell. You know what I mean, pretty baby?

Adrian Stanford

(1950? – 1981)

Adrian Stanford, a native of Philadelphia, is the author of a chapbook entitled
Black and Queer *(Good Gay Poets Press of Boston, 1977), a book
considered the first collection of queer poetry published by a black man. Adrian
was murdered on July 21, 1981. His date of birth appears uncertain.*

i love much
therefore i am greatly despised
yet as i am hated
so shall i be adored

Sacrifice

had my father known
when he cast forth his offering
to the sea of my mother's womb
what creation their joy would bring
would he have welcomed the man / she child in its birth
heralding my duality as nature's zenith (in human form)
and blessed the son he held for all to see
keeping my sister / self obscured, until
i understood my second destiny—
or would he have shuddered at the fate his loins possessed
and retracting from those clashing thighs,
let the seeds that bore such strains
meet their end upon the ground

Statement

if the realm of our magnificence is oblivious to you,
observe with keener eyes those you taunt and defame
with such vigorous animosity.
we have been forced to shame ourselves
in the restrooms and alleyways of your cities
because you deny us the privilege of consorting openly
with our own kind.
we are creatures of love and dreaming.
our birthright : a handsome face to kiss away melancholy tears
and husband the fragility of our incandescent lives.
at best, we are the phantoms of your would-be dreams.
at worst, the childishness of forgotten days
that you discarded,
for the amber cloak of maturity.

In the darkness, fuck me now
for Donald Thomas Williams

In the darkness, fuck me now.
speak not, for the rustling of white linen
will make music,
and the occasional zooming of cars
below will add to the rhapsody,
and as silence, deep and pregnant, settles
in our ears (taking us beyond lust's ocean roar),
we will drift on our minds' eternal sea.
falling stars will be our witness. the wetness
of my loins proclaims the rite.
i am pinioned in your arms. silent, and hard breathing.
each breathing creates galaxies; where unnamed
children call me god—
and shout in their private gloom, as i do:
fuck me now.

for sonny cozzi

wait in some un/discovered corner
where no man has profaned
the sweetness that is love
and i will come at sun's setting
to kiss away your fears
and hold your strong hand
in my own

David Bergman

(1950 –

David Bergman splits his time between teaching, scholarship, essay writing, editing and poetry. His most recent passion is gardening; his most sustained passion is his partner of nearly fifteen years. He teaches in the English department of Towson State University, and serves as theater critic for The City Paper, *Baltimore.*

The Guide of Tiresias

"I think of Oedipus, old, led by a boy"—Thom Gunn

Never was there a time when I did not lead him,
when I did not feel his hand upon my shoulder.

Never was there a time I was not his eyes
to tell him here lies Thebes, and there stands Corinth,

here the rocks have given way, and there two snakes coil
like twisted rope looking for a neck to hang on.

Sometimes I thought he was my mother, so gently
did he hold me when I was sick, so tenderly

did he wash me at the end of a long journey,
when he could barely stand, his arms stiff and shrivelled.

Sometimes I thought he might be my father, so strong
was his grip on my body to keep me from danger,

so firm his warnings, so stern his admonitions.
And then at times he was my child, and hungrily

fed on my warmth and caresses, afraid of what
others—burning with questions—might force him to say.

"What will happen to us?" he would cry at nightfall
as if he did not already know the answer.

The Psalm of Prometheus

"Throughout the happy Golden Age, only men
were upon the earth; there were no women.
Zeus created these later, in his anger at
Prometheus for caring so much for men . . ."
                                        —*Edith Hamilton*

"What do gods eat?" he asked,
although he wasn't hungry.

They eat the tender edges of your ears, I answered,
the bloody rosettes of your nipples.

He scowled: "I am tired of fruit and crushed oats,
gnarled roots and the juice of ripened berries."

So I brought him the meats he wanted,
the pale loins of calves,

the shanks of mothering ewes,
birds plucked and gutted from the sky,

and he let me lick the back of his neck
and chew the space between his shoulder blades.

"How do the gods eat this?" he asked me, spitting out the raw
flesh, which was tough and stringy and impossible to chew.

We warm it first in the heat of our desire, I answered,
we sear it in the flames of passion.

"I'm sick of cold mutton," he shouted,
throwing aside his helpings of uncooked goat and venison.

So I brought him fire,
which crackled like trampled twigs and hissed like startled cobra.

Only then did he let me feast on his body
until we both were sated.

Zeus, master of revenge,
no torture you'd have fashioned

could have inflicted more exquisite pain
nor brought my spirit lower—

not the chains that bite my skin as once I teethed on his,
not the mountain to which I'm bound as once I held him fast,

not even the eagle who plucks my liver through the wounds that
cannot heal—no, none of these could have brought the torment

of watching him flail each night
with that woman you created at his side,

her pudgy fingers fluttering with pleasure
above her tightly-lidded box.

The Blueberry Man

I was never the one to spot him walking
slowly up the street, pulling his yellow
wagon. It was always a brother or sister
who'd race home with the news. Then everything
spun into action like gulls at low tide.

Mother would shoo the children from the yard
and hide us out of danger in the living room,
warning with harsh whispers not to peek
from the windows and knowing we would anyway,
tracking the blueberry man across the porch
to where he knocked at the kitchen door.

Grandfather greeted him. Mother said
she was afraid. But I think she was jealous.
For though I was five or six, I knew I'd
never see such beautiful hair again. Hair
like a storybook princess. Great golden skeins,
falling halfway down his back. And such eyes,
freaked like a robin's egg and bobbing
beneath mascara waves of lashes. I remember
the Victory Red lips unfurling like a flag
when he spoke and the frilly shirt.

My brothers
giggled nervously. But I wasn't scared.
I wanted to pull the chiffon curtains back
and speak. But what would I say? That I knew
what it was to be alone? That I had heard
my own family scamper with trepidation
from my door when I was quarantined with
scarlet fever and no one but my mother was
allowed into my room?
I could have said:
I'm only a child but certain to end an outcast too.
Still, I said nothing, except once, a weak
goodby for which I was roundly scolded.
I used to ride my bike to his house, a tiny
cabin covered with angry brambles and
the hiss of intriguing bees, hoping we'd meet.
But he stayed inside during the day when he
wasn't peddling the wares he gathered at night.

One sleepless dawn I saw him coming home
with a kerosene lantern in one hand
and a silvery pail in the other.
Mother washed his berries twice to cleanse
them of his memory, as if he communicated
with his touch the fearful urge to dress
in women's clothing. For dessert she'd douse
the fruit with milk or pile them on peaks of
sour cream, chubby mountain climbers in the snow.
My brothers ate them greedily. But I
when everyone had left the table, would
still be seated, savoring the sweet juice
and the delicate flesh he had brought me.

A Part for Horn

I don't recall his name, but his death
made all the papers. In the school yard
we passed around forbidden copies
of the *Daily News* with photographs—

that back alley where he was found,
the outline of his naked body
barely visible beneath the sheet.

For a moment even the fat girls
with smudged blue eye-shadow stopped giggling,
and the black kids, who leapt like dolphins
beneath the basketball hoops, hung fire;
Latinos, who reigned by divine right
in the handball courts, instinctively
bowed their heads and crossed their hard torsos.

Since he was new at school, he was made
a third trumpet in our concert band.
From my vantage in the sax section
I could observe his pale face darken
as he blew hard into the mouthpiece.
Once Mr. Vitalli ordered him to stand
and play the sad legato

of Moussorgsky's *"Great Gate of Kiev"*
which traditionally had begun
our spring program. Anxiously we watched
as his fingers trembled on the valves
and the flat notes sputtered and cracked. But
with the piece done, he bowed so gravely
that the whole class burst into applause.

Even Mr. Vitalli, whose aim
had been to humiliate him, saw
that here was a student whose in-born
sense of the absurd placed him beyond
the restraints of shame and honor
or other cheap pedagogic tricks
with which our teachers were familiar.

But also it freed him from the need
for admiration. The perfect child,
lithe as a whippet, whose seal-slick thatch
of hair slung low across his eye lids,
was indifferent to all about him
though ready to carry on his back
the world's weight or the heavier void.

I wish I could give you a picture
of him as he sat alone, later, waiting
for Mr. Vitalli's cue and not
the grade school graduation photo
published in *The Times* with hair combed back,
an unfocused smile blurring his face,
two passionless and babyish eyes.

I wish a camera had been there
to catch him as I saw him: a Jew
whose skin was as luminous and pure
as a page of the Torah before
the flame—like letters scorch across it,
with lips made sensuous and firm
by a faith in unfulfilled desire.

None of us knew what homeroom he had,
though surely one with the slowest boys
from which he'd rise to attend Music.
A friend once had him in gym where he
always emerged last from the shower
as though he had lost his way in the steam.
At lunch he disappeared completely.

He never ate, though once I saw him
in the darkest corner of the yard,
wrapped in an old herringbone topcoat
that hung down to his feet. There pigeons
devotedly pecked bits of sandwich
until a gust of wind blew open
his coat, and he took wing like a god.

Later the homicide detective
spoke of the need for information
and left behind a number to call
if we could remember any clues:
a name he might have mentioned, a stray
remark he might have made,
a stranger who might have met him at the gate.

But it was useless for him to ask.
We had reached that age when all our loves
were secrets kept even from ourselves
whose desires of unspeakable
proportions were held in bounds by fear
and ignorance of what might bring them
abatement if not satisfaction.

Nor could we explain how one of us
had courage enough to leave his home
for the embrace of men lured to bars,
the uncertainty of their kindness,
the unfamiliar, unmade beds, which
having filled the momentary need,
are left the morning after vacant.

Nor could I admit the guilt I felt
was a kind of vanity, for what
I wanted to confess to him would
not have changed his fate. Had I told him
how I dreamt at night of his fingers
playing upon me, pressing my skin
like the ivory keys of his trumpet,

his cheeks flushed from the sound that rose up
from my throat—he still would have run off
into the inconsolable night
to give his body to thankless men
and fall through the cracks of the city,
and still the papers would drop his tale
and leave the murder as yet unsolved.

Though twenty years have passed, I often
will think of him when I find myself
afraid with a stranger beside me,
when I watch children in the school yard
playing, or when, as tonight, I hear
faintly from a distance, a student
up in his room practicing the horn.

Vytautas Pliura

(1951 –

Vytautas Pliura grew up in a farm town in Southern Illinois and is first generation Lithuanian. He received a degree from UCLA in Motion Picture Production and worked as a screenwriter until discovering poetry. He resides in Los Angeles, where he is just completing his first novel.

In the Hands of the Enemy

Their skin was ivory
The jungle was emerald
They kept me in a bamboo cage
I was given, quite mysteriously, a
    mahogany chair to sit in
A strange privilege

Because I was known to be gay
    they let me grow orchids in my cell
Orchids don't lust after much light
I also fed the monkeys and the peacocks
    and was let out to make rice paper at the
    blind woman's hut

Often
when a South Vietnamese prisoner was to be
    executed
that prisoner could request to humiliate a
    prisoner from the USA by making him give
    the condemned person
    oral sex

Mark and Willard both had jet black hair
    and did not impress the Montagnards
One mountain man traveled 250 kilometers to
    cut off some of my blonde ringlets to
    weave into dolls for his children

I, blue-eyed Central Illinois farm boy a
    little speck of purple-mountain-majesty among the
    hobbled rubber trees and the elf-like golden
    shimmering teak trees
    was led into a clearing

The prisoner to be shot was tied to a post, I could
    hear the women washing their clothes in the Red River
    singing lullabyes

        Hands tied behind my back
        I was lowered to my knees

    One boy shot his semen down my throat as he lurched with
    bullets

Loins quivering
It took him ten minutes to die
It took them that long to free his fingers
    from my hair

These Aren't the Boys I Got Butterflies in My Stomach Over

I go to a gay bar
I look around

These aren't the boys I got butterflies in my stomach over

In high school
On the track team
In the marching band
In the science club

These boys
Don't resemble
Bruce Owens
or
Jimmy Heberling
or Leland Dehm
with their Huckleberry Finn grins

In math class
I could not concentrate
because
Steve Epperson
sat in front of me

I looked at his thick black hair
As thick as a table top

In the gay bar
I look around

They are haughty, fake, malevolent
Now in their underpants at these underwear parties,
chiseled, phony, blown-up gym bodies,
    mean-looking
Who wants to see a bunch of fags in their underpants?

These are not the boys
I got butterflies in my stomach over

Where did they go?

Scott

I spoke to a very young boy in a bar
He said, "Wanna go to your place?"

We got in my Chevy, cherry red.
He looked like a movie star. Thick black hair. Like Matt
    Dillon.

"How old are you?" I said.
"Where do you live?" he said.
"Not far."
"My mother died today."
"I'm sorry."
"Look, the moon looks like a cheap earring. L.A. is cool,
    man."

The only thing I had in the house to drink was Tang.
When he took off his preppie cream-colored coat I noticed he
    had a tattoo of a dragon with one fang.

"Where's the bedroom?"
"Would you like some Tang?"
"Cool, man."

He turned on my radio to a station playing Bach.

He took off his pants.

He had a beautiful cock.
"Wanna fuck on the floor?" he said.
"I was hoping for more."
"Like what, man?"
"I guess I wanted to talk a little."

He took off his football jersey.

I noticed fresh razor cuts up and down both arms.

Still bleeding.

His chest was mutilated with cuts.
He had used a knife to cut a large heart on his chest.

"What happened to your arms?"

"My mother's death, you know,
I broke up with my boyfriend the other day, too.
A lot of things.
A zebra wouldn't eat outta my hand at the zoo,
    he was cool with everyone but me. I haven't had Tang for
    years, man.
They drank this in outer space."

We made love on the rug.
Okay we fucked on the floor.

I discovered he'd mutilated his penis.

After his orgasm he trembled like a deer I once ran over on

a Wisconsin highway, the beautiful tan buck lay there
twitching and dying in a ditch with tiny antlers coming
out of his head.

I gave him my jar of Tang.

It wasn't until after he left that I realized he'd cut
    himself up to resemble the striped zebra that refused to
    eat from his hand.

I realized that the scars he wore openly on the outside
I wore on the inside.

Thomas

I believe the hardest thing I ever did
was coping with the fact, growing up,
that I was in love with my brother

He was five years younger
and his shoulder blades changed from balsa wood airplane
wings into a ship's mast in the eighth grade year
Under each of his arms was the beginning of a robin's nest

He slept in his underpants, sheetless, the moon watching us like a
restless nun, in a bed a body's length away from me
His skin was ivory
His curly chestnut-colored hair slept on his forehead
He looked like the boy on the Grecian urn in my
textbook at school
He was my brother
I wanted to take him in my arms and make passionate
love to him

In the summer we baled hay together
We herded cattle together
We swam in the pond together
seeing who could hold their breath the longest
I drove him in town to the Piggly Wiggly so he could
buy his race car magazines

I drove him to the new Dairy Queen on the new highway so
he could buy a pineapple malt
We laughed at dirty jokes
He would take off his T-shirt as we sped down the back roads
Central Illinois farms would whiz by us like a green-
colored Oz
His hard chest looked like butterscotch
Sweat glistened on his body like diamonds
I wanted to lick them off

I hated myself
I felt like a pervert
I felt like an assassin
I felt like a man moments away from the gallows
His eyes were as green as the pond on a bright, cloudless
June afternoon

I watched his buttocks move in his jeans
I watched his square jaw eat the oatmeal I'd fix him in the
morning
He was as beautiful as our walnut grove
He was as beautiful as Huckleberry Finn
He was as beautiful as a warm spring rain
He was as spunky as the wind that kept up our homemade kites
He was my brother

How do you tell your fourteen year old brother you want to
kiss him on the mouth until the world ends and the angels
rest in our maple trees

He looked up to me as a hero
I was president of the senior class
I was starring in the senior play
I had the 4th fastest two-mile in McLean county

I wanted to put my face on his chest and travel to a world as yet
undiscovered by explorers
Perhaps his chest was the surface of the moon
There was a mystery in his taut little man-boy chest, butterscotch
flavored, that would rival all the mysteries of Egypt
I had a dream he had, in a former life, been sacrificed to a Pharaoh
I wanted to eat his soul

I wanted to...........

It was these feelings that pushed me toward suicide.

Nobody in their right mind falls in love with their younger brother.

I felt filthy
Rodent-like
I may as well have eaten the mud pies Thomas and I made after a
violent spring shower, the rich Illinois loam soil as black as a moonless
midnight

I rocked him in my arms for hours that first day my parents brought
him home from the hospital

I was almost five

My brother
My brother
My brother
Rocking Rocking   Rocking   Until the end of the world

I felt I had given birth to him
He was as big as a football
He cried when I stopped rocking

Angels in the maple trees

He was a mystery
What was he going to become

If it had just been sexual desire I may have been able to cope and tuck
it away in an appropriate coffin

But I was feverishly in love with him
I was obsessed with him like early man was obsessed with the sun

My body ached for him in the night
Our bodies as close to each other
as two soldiers who had killed each other in a trench
Toy soldiers papered our bedroom walls
The moon looked in through the shutters, blinking like a senile, old,
ruby-eyed, judging nun

One night
I got up from my bed
and I stood over him
His face was crushed into his pillow
as vulnerable as a girl

I had to know what his buttocks felt like
I lay my hand on his thigh, through his underpants
like a museum guard reaching out for a statue
It lasted all of thirty seconds
He was made of elephant tusk.

I returned to my bed

The next afternoon my father called me into his room
"Last night did you touch your brother?"
It was the end of the world

Thomas had not been asleep
I was turned in
Like Nazi children turn in their parents
I tasted vomit in my mouth
My father smoked cigarette after cigarette
Shaking like a cocker spaniel that had been kicked he
choked on his Old Golds
The end of the world was now
The angels watched from low branches of the maple trees
their wings beating as though they were underwater
"Yes, I did."
The angels looked at me sternly, also smoking
Old Gold cigarettes
nervously

My father suggested a psychiatrist
I was the golden boy turned into a slimy eel

My father was more jittery than angry
His hands missed his mouth several times in an attempt to smoke his
cigarette
He was wearing a beautiful three-piece suit
I never saw him in anything but a dark, three-piece suit
I think he slept in his three-piece suit

He was a surgeon
He could slice into people's brains
but he could not deal with his son

The angels languished in the maple trees, wearing three-piece suits,
blowing smoke rings, double smoke rings that transformed themselves
into Thomas' buttocks

A darkness overtook me
I walked around in a daze
Soon my mother would know
The angels were whispering among themselves
This was the end of the world
I was one of Columbus' sailors and my ship fell off the edge of the
world
I felt I was falling through darkness so dark it was God
The angels watched uncaringly as I hurled down into
Satan's jaws
Numb   A sinner falling through the hands of an angry God
Dead   A corpse on the shore of the Sea of Tranquility
Without hope
Exiled from Eden, I had touched the forbidden marble statue, flecked
with topaz and gold
Mindreaders
They knew I wanted to drink the saliva of an angel

The night before I was to go to see the psychiatrist
I took a bottle of sleeping pills from my father's bathroom
I went to bed feeling dizzy and sick and happy, contented
I saw my brother stretched out on his bed like a mummy
He had pulled the covers up over himself tightly
That whole week he hadn't said two words to me
The apocalypse had arrived

All I thought was
"At least I don't have to spend another night lying next to him, lusting
like a rabid dog.

This will be my last."

I wasn't the least bit afraid of dying.
I was relieved.
I was at peace.

I had eaten the entire bottle of pills as if they were M&M's.
I laid my head on my pillow, serene, thankful.
A delicious feeling crept over me like someone pouring bubble bath over me. Thomas' face floated by like a
crystal ball.

I began to lift away like a child's balloon escaping from the child.
I was thankful that it was all over.

Then the pills began to pull at me like dragon's claws.
I remembered Thomas in his Casper the Friendly Ghost Halloween costume when he was ten.
He held out his trick-or-treat bag to me. We were swimming in the pond naked during an electrical storm. We were riding in the pickup, he threw his malt out the window. I was kissing him on the mouth in the barn. I was rocking him as a baby.

My baby brother.
My baby brother.

I woke up in the hospital with a tube down my nose that hurt like hell.
My stomach was being pumped.

Thomas had awakened my parents because I was vomiting in my sleep.

My father was very angry that I should "try such a stunt."
I told him that I was even angrier.
I told him I was angry to be alive.
I spit in his face.
He, the man dressed in the three-piece suit.
He, the god-like doctor.
He, sperm-maker of Thomas and me.
I watched the spit roll down his cheek.
Then I gagged on the hose in my nose.
The nurses soon turned into angels in three-piece suits smoking Old Gold cigarettes. The smell of maple leaves was everywhere.

Thomas came to visit me.

He stood there like the boy on the Grecian urn.
I was as cold as the stone urn he was made of. I did not speak to him.
I rang the nurse to remove him. "I love you," he said. He began to cry.
He tried to hug me.

I heaved him away. The intravenous needle broke in my arm.
The urn broke.
Shattered on the floor.
An orderly who looked like Rumpelstiltskin breezed in and swept up
the fragile pieces. Outside the clouds rolled by like elephant kings.

I was taken away to a mental institution where I drew watercolors and
occasionally saw a doctor who looked like President Garfield after he
was shot.
There were three women who each thought they were Joan of Arc and
continually fought with each other like alley cats, calling the others
impostors.

I think Frances was the real Joan of Arc.
She did the most convincing recreation of being burned alive.

Occasionally we took a bus trip to go bowling.
Nothing more hilarious than a bunch of mental patients bowling.
Frances wore her rented bowling shoes home on purpose because they
were more comfortable than her institution shoes.

I had shock treatments.
I did not recognize Thomas when I got home. I did not know my
sisters or my mother or my father.

Now, these many years later, Thomas is a doctor, handsome as ever.
We are friends.
He hugs me a lot when I visit.
He has full-fledged robin's nests under his arms.

Dan Bellm

(1952 –

Born in Springfield, Illinois, Dan Bellm lives in San Francisco with his partner and seven-year-old son. His sequence of poems about fatherhood and his own father is launching the new California Poetry Series from Roundhouse Press, Berkeley, and a second collection is coming out from Cleveland State University Press in the fall of 1999.

Transfigured

I was pushing my baby in the stroller up Market St.
when I passed the open door of the room you and I
made love in one slow afternoon so long ago it appeared to me
as a photograph of a doorway in a building
that's been torn down for years and replaced
with another structure. A maid's cart was waiting on the sidewalk
with brooms and disinfectants like the angel
that removes from empty rooms the history
of the human beings who have lived in them,
their gestures and cries. The baby was exuberant
as he is these days almost all his waking hours,
gripping the handlebar face up to the sun and rocking
forward and back to make the world go faster,
squealing with the anticipation of a roller coaster dip
in the terrain of his existence about to stir him more alive
at every moment. The unadorned walls
and the bedspread printed with cowboy hats and pistols and ropes
made it look like the lonely room I shared with my brother
but transfigured for a moment by our boyish light and sweat,
our comical rendezvous to be alone there
where no one would know us, your breath in my ear
asking, Will you be my brother? It is hours in the future
where you are now in a country an ocean away
but I could see the little infinite spiral of the rumpled sheets
and the bedside lamp still lit against the motionless
dark, just as we left it when we had to step back

into the afternoon of an ordinary day and walk each other
to the corner to say goodbye, too ignorant of forever
to spend tears on it. Happiness comes eventually to me
but only on condition that sadness come first,
and since I had been quiet too long
and distracted from our babbling song of the constantly moving city
the baby turned around in the stroller with an inquisitive smile
to look at me.

from **Book of Maps**

If I'm not a strong person—if I'm not like other
boys—maybe I shouldn't have been a boy
at all. In his halflit room the child
is looking at his body
with his brand-new glasses off. Here
he can be as invisible as he wants. Yes,

it's getting harder to see; yes,
his vision will be bad forever; yes, the others
will outrace him as he feels his way. Here,
held up a little closer than before, are a girl's
hands, not the hands of his father—anybody
can see how the bones could break. Sensitive child—

oversensitive—you can't let the other children
make you cry his mother says—*Ignore them, yes,*
that's what I did in school. He wishes his body
could be solider or disappear when the other
boys come at him at the schoolyard door, one boy
in particular who spits, says *faggot* and *girl,* who hit him here

in the chest until he did cry, and here
on his girl-limp arms. His body is not his hope. The child
supposes if he were a girl
the other boys might like him then, yes,
might even apologize, and he would like the other
boys to care for him, one in particular whose body

is mean and shines with sweat, him more than anybody,
and the child touches himself here
where his legs join while the other
hand strokes the rising—um—the child
doesn't yet call it anything to himself—yes—
until he shivers to a stop, imagining the boy

beside him, *but I would have to be a girl*
for that, and I'm not, I have this puny body
of a boy. Then hope must lie in his mind, yes,
all right, he can see more clearly in here
with his bad eyes shut, this child
who would rather have any other

body but his own, a girlboy
given to see the world as through a glass, but here
is his body and he will live in it, yes, because there is no other.

Boy wearing a dress

On the way home he asks me, *If we cut off our*
penises then we'd be girls wouldn't we Dad,
my little boy in cowboy boots and a long black dress
walking home from Castro Street playing
blue fairy and wicked stepsister and lost princess as he
walks, the people and store windows whirling by

as he twirls only figures in fairy stories he knows by
heart, though what he doesn't see yet is that our
neighborhood's a kind of fairyland for real—still, I hope no one heard
him ask me that, and hope my Dad
who is dead hasn't heard, who would never have let me play
boy and girl with this frightening freedom, dressing

up in public or alone in a four-dollar thrift-store dress
we bought because he asked for one. A drunk careening by
asks, *Why who are you some kind of superhero, son,* and from a display
window video porno stars sweating under harsh light smirk in our
faces—*I don't have to tell them who I am now do I Dad*—
No it's a dress, the guy's friend says, *I've seen him*

around before, that boy's always in costume, he
must be a little fag. Ken dolls in white satin dresses
and angel wings and hairless Barbies done up as leather Dads
are climbing a Christmas tree inside the card shop by
the pizza store, some queen's fantasy scenario of what our
mothers and fathers should have let us play

back where we come from, but my little boy likes to play
the girl parts of stories for reasons of his own, he
likes their speeches and their dresses and shoes, we tell ourselves
it's harmless, wanting to wear a dress,
harmless as my nervous laughter to passersby
and what do I apologize to them for, Dad—

When I was a child I wanted to wear my Dad's
work shirts, I liked the smell of his Army uniform, I didn't play
girl games, don't look at me. My little boy is getting distracted by
the dildoes at the sex shop I try to hustle him past. Soon enough he'll
learn to leave his dress at home, will hear somewhere that a boy in a dress
cannot be beautiful. Once inside our

house he undresses by the mirror to be naked under the dress,
and lifts it up to display what most of us keep inside our
pants, and he asks me, a little afraid for the answer, *Am I beautiful, Dad—*

Dennis Cooper

(1953 –

A native of Pasadena, California, Dennis Cooper is a poet of four collections,
editor, essayist, critic, anthologist, and soon to publish his fifth novel. If all goes
as planned, next year he will be writing and directing his first porn film.
He lives in the Los Feliz hills in Southern California.

Greg Tomeoni

I was in Eighth grade
when we was in Seventh.
He bought Dylan the same day
I did, and wanted
to sleep with me (he called
it frigging), so we tried.
His breath was of hamburger
and I licked his teeth
when he kissed me.
He held my wrist,
serious as a doctor.
He was dark and Italian, energetic
and long haired. He liked
his boys tall and thin, like him.
I was the first of millions, he said.
I remember our position,
side by side, and the quick pulse
of our breaths, sometimes
steady, sometimes off on their own
like two men racing.
I remember him saying he loved me
and that I thanked him
and that we didn't cum (too young I think)
but grew bored of it around sunrise
turning back to back, smoking,
filling the room with
a pale cloud, a food smell.
We slept in a hot blue night.

Mark Clark

walked with his hands
near his hips
like he wore guns
and was Wanted
in fifty states.

Out of the blue
something would tic him
and he'd attack
a friend, a girl,
whatever was near,
his face dark
as a rag pushed
onto a wound.
He was so alive then;
you had to desire
his wildness, his looks.

Even the coaches
let him pound
and bought him beers afterwards
and wanted to run him
for a week, train him,
be the one to bring him down.
And I, too,
in my room at night
dreamt of taming him
with my body, my mouth
so wet he would drink from it
like a kid does a hose
when he has been running all day
and must stop, must drink.

Scott Van Der Karr

It was the Christmas dance
wasn't it? My rock band
played. You joined the dance floor.
We had knocked over the big tree.
We had opened the mock packages.
Some of us were stoned, and
festooned our hair with the wrapping.
The stink of our two bit colognes
filled the air, sweetest at the dancing.
It was light only in blemishes.
We were moving, that was all.
It vanished behind and ahead of us.
My band was the Stones. I, Jagger.
Your eyes were closed. You knew your way.
You wore an old pair of jeans
and fringe jacket tight
at the back, vague at the front.
Cocks didn't matter then.
It was ass we dreamed of, smooth as our ideas.
You knew how to wear yours.
Girls took it in their hands
when they danced. It rose through them;
it gripped their breasts;
it glowed out their eyes and mouths.
Though you were stoned
and stumbling, braying your words,
every girl schemed for you,
cute as you were, and steeped in blonde.
Now my cock was up like Jim Morrison's,
your name mixed with Nadine's.
I sang the songs to you: the rough and
hard ones, the silky ballads.
Later I danced beside you, drunken,
stumbled into you again and again.
And I could smell your sweat and your breath.
Everyone could. Did you notice?

Steve Nelson

The beauty I saw in
him was a cross
between Marilyn Monroe
and shade.
It shared my beers
and my sleep
through high school.
In those days
his thinness graced
every ball game
with its fumbling
and his face
without a care.
I pointed him out to Lisa
and she wanted him
like a dog wants human hands
(her analogy).
She had an advantage,
being a girl,
and screwed her way
through his friends
("wimps and monsters")
to reach him one night
in the ruins of some party
when he was too drunk,
saw breasts in the fog of his eyes
and drooped to them
gulping back vomit and weakness.
She had to strip him down,
bite his cock hard,
bang his thin ass.
"Still, it was the best screw
ever, ...there could possibly be,"
she smiled
smoking his Marlboros.
My cock raged in my jeans,
attesting to the fact;
but, I begged to differ.

First Sex

This isn't it.
I thought it would be
Like having a boned pillow.

I saw myself turning
over and over in lust
like sheets in a dryer.

My style was reckless,
wool dry. Other than mine
there were little or no arms.

I could whisper anything
into an implied ear
and praise would rise
like a colorless, scentless gas.
Then I would breathe to sleep.

But my lover moves.
And my lips grow numb as rubber
before I capture half the ass
that rose like Atlantis
from my dreams.

I try to get his shoulder blade between my teeth
He complains, pillow in his mouth.
Doesn't mean it.
Means it.

He rolls onto his back,
face raw and wet as fat,
like it has been shaken from nightmares.
I don't know how to please this face.

Tomorrow when he has made breakfast
and gone, I will sweep
the mound of porno from my closet,
put a match to its lies.

I will wait in my bed
as I did before, a thought ajar,

and sex will slip into my room
like a white tiger.

David Cassidy Now
bathroom, Male Man Theater

He's a little faggier
than you expected
but cute as your sister
thought he was, way
back before love.

But it's you
he's after, asking a match.
"Hey," he smiles,
"I was on tv once."
You know, you say.

What would your
sister do? Cry?
Nah, she'd probably
tell her friends
and have a big laugh.

You want to refuse him
but you can't;
he's still the face
that brought girls' tongues
to his pages in magazines.

Now it's your turn,
pressing your tongue
to the sweaty actuality
while other men
dream of your luck.

When one kingdom falls
another rises.
So now it's gays

who flock around "The
Partridge Family"

and buy the albums
no girl would touch.
Now David is ours
to moan about, and to find
like gold in these dark caves.

High School Basketball
for Steve Hufsteter

When boys wanted to toss the ball around they'd use ninth period
when nothing was going on. I'd see a herd of them heading down the
gym stairs. I'd join them if no one had brought any Hendrix records or
dope. I'd be in the middle of that crowd, trampling the steps like water
in front of a busted dam. We'd hit the cool of the locker room. We
couldn't stop moving around, too ready. Jock strap never washed. Short
blue trunks. Blue tee-shirt or not. Dirty white socks to our knees.
Tennis shoes (white or black) with our names. You remember. And a
graham cracker stink in the towels. Scott, who dressed near me, had the
best body and smiled all the time. I think he liked my body, which was
o.k. then, pale but tight. Anyway, we were all stripping, a nice feeling,
freedom, sort of warm around me. Then we were laughing, chasing the
ball down court. Sometimes there'd be a few girls in the bleachers talking boys with their faces close together. Only the best girls hung
around the gym this late. It was sexy to be talked about and we'd get
hard and glad we were clamped in the jock strap. We could grow full
size but they'd never see it. Christ, those girls begged for it. We kept
fucking up thinking about them. The game came and went, then we'd
stuff the shower room, two in one, brushing up against one another still
hard under the spray. Skin's so great under water. It's good to touch
anyone then, especially when you're talking about chicks like we were,
measuring out tits with our hands. We'd look at each other and get
harder until one of us played with himself. Then we'd laugh, lean back
against the walls and jack off while the steam puffed from sharp sprays
and our hair curled. Some girl walking by would have knelt before that
white world, forbidding as Neptune's. And writing this I have grown
harder than I have in years, and the couch sticks to my back like the
tiles did, sort of asking me to stay there, stay young. I wish we had.

Jim Cory

(1953 –

*Jim Cory lives in the City of Brotherly Love, where he supports himself
and several cats as a freelance writer. He has published numerous essays, articles,
stories, reviews, edited several major collections of poetry, and is a founding
member of Insight to Riot, a poet's press based in Philadelphia.*

Wife

"Oh oh," she said. "Button missing.
You want me sew?"

That would be very nice, I said.

Outside the light changed:
#12 bus blew fumes
thru the door of Park Hung Cleaners.

"How come wife no do?
Wife working?"

No wife, I said.

With knit brow she unrolled sleeves.
"In Korea all man have wife."

She scratched out *5 shirts
No Starch, Hangers*
on the slip, wrote my name
across the top
in ball point pen smiling.

"You live by self? No family?"

Yes, I said. By myself.
With 4 cats. Off the street.

"Oh, cats. I allergic."
She scratched her arm
& feigned a sneeze.
We both giggled.

"How come American man no want wife?"

she said, handing the slip
over a worn wood counter
piled with pants skirts shirts

& then a thought crossed her face
& she said:

"Ooooooohh. You prefer the man?"

I folded the slip once, twice
4 times pushed it
deep in my wallet.

Yes, I told her, I prefer the man.

"All you life? From this big?" she said
making waist-high gesture.

I smiled, admiring
her directness & nodded.

"I no understand this.
Never go with woman?"

Many years ago, I told her.
Enough to know
what was right
for myself.

"That too bad for me," she said.
"American husband hard to find."

We giggled again.

I told her
I couldn't agree more.

bodybuilder

his protein milkshakes his fistfuls of vitamins

his razored scalp & blond mustache

his highschoolkid clothes

the elegant meat architecture of his arms

the times he danced shirtless in clubs & went home
      to sleep alone

the times he entrained for New York & never heard the opera

the times he benchpressed twice his own weight

his eyes that asked *why* then repeated the question

his personal ad: "sober BB who also writes poetry seeks
      similar..."

his 2nd floor brownstone studio posters & shelved sets of Tolstoy

his refusal to own a TV

the time he caked his face with oatmeal to erase the lines

the time his only creditcard was seized buying rollerskates
      at the ArmyNavy

the time he tumbled from bed laughing at someone's penis & said
      years later *I know now we pay for everything we do*

the mouthful of teeth he left in a crushed VW

the winged things that flew thru him

his sunshade Walkman silence disguise & phone unanswered

his fat tin toad of a typewriter anchoring drafts & unpaid bills

his 1 published poem his hundred flaming bridges

his memory of perfect love of nightwhispered teenage underwear
    stirrings

his bathroom mirror the dimesized purplish islands on his back

his 2 years doctors hospitals drugs tests & transfusions

the time he lost his race with incontinence on Broad St.

the poem he wrote about it

the TV he agreed to take the male nurse nattering in the bathroom
    the mousesized roach under the fridge the fridge filled with
    everything he couldn't eat/drink/lift

his scalded limp paw & infant hair

his telescope spectacles

his voice full of sand & abandoned nests

his final sigh

the fullmoon silence of its echo

the row of parked cars on the hill

the brass box resting on Astroturf

his jacketed photo in promtux toppled in sudden breeze

Memoir: Spring, '77

He drove over
a low stone wall
parked the Dart

far out
in an unplowed field.
We cleared

the junk off the back
pushed the seats
down & got

naked.
It went on
for some hours

& when we were thru
sticky with sweat
& the white runny

stuff he called
"boy-butter"
we sat there, smoking

nude in the huge
nightquiet.
"Let's go," he said.

We pulled on our clothes.
The Dart lurched
halted

whirred up mud
& went
nowhere.

We left it
under a late May moon
got back the next day

to find
fresh–turned earth
& the Dart

plowed all around.
From the field's far side
we saw its owner

astride a great green tractor.
He rumbled toward us.
"Hello fellas," he said

& offered a tow.
We roped the bumper
to the hitch

& had it out
in a minute.
Thank you, we said.

"Hope she was good," he said.
We said
she was.

Mark Doty

(1953 –

Mark Doty and his partner, Paul Lisicky, a novelist, live in Provincetown during the spring and summer, in an 18th century house a block from the harbor. Mark has five published collections of verse, a recently completed memoir, and teaches each fall in the creative writing program at the University of Houston. He's an aficionado of dogs, gardens, fabric, weightlifting, tattoos, and the ways in which people reinvent themselves, making their mark on the world—from outsider artists to drag queens.

The Death of Antinoüs

When the beautiful young man drowned—
accidentally, swimming at dawn
in a current too swift for him,
or obedient to some cult
of total immersion that promised
the bather would come up divine,

mortality rinsed from him—
Hadrian placed his image everywhere,
a marble Antinoüs staring across
the public squares where a few dogs
always scuffled, planted
in every squalid little crossroad

at the farthest corners of the Empire.
What do we want in any body
but the world? And if the lover's
inimitable form was nowhere,
then he would find it everywhere,
though the boy became simply more dead

as the sculptors embodied him.
Wherever Hadrian might travel,
the beloved figure would be there

first: the turn of his shoulders,
the exact marble nipples,
the drowned face not really lost

to the Nile—which has no appetite,
merely takes in anything
without judgment or expectation—
but lost into its own multiplication,
an artifice rubbed with oils and acid
so that the skin might shine.

Which of these did I love?
Here is his hair, here his hair
again. Here the chiseled liquid waist
I hold because I cannot hold it.
If only one of you, he might have said
to any of the thousand marble boys anywhere,

would speak. Or the statues might have been enough,
the drowned boy blurred as much by memory
as by water, molded toward an essential,
remote ideal. Longing, of course,
becomes its own object, the way
that desire can make anything into a god.

63rd Street Y

All night steam heat pours
from radiators and up the stairwells
to the thirteenth floor,
and I can't sleep because I know
all the windows are thrown wide open,

a voyeur's advent calendar.
If I lean out the screenless frame
the building's twin flanks yield
banks of lit rectangles above a black courtyard
where a few papers lie completely still,

this warm December. Thirteen dizzying stories
show tonight and any night some blank shades
or black glass, and dozens of interiors—
men all right, mostly not young
or strikingly Christian, though certainly associated.

The nude black man two windows over
is lying in bed, Melchior halfway
through his journey, writing a letter home.
And on the twelfth floor, in my favorite window,
only a little corner holding

the foot of the bed visible,
a pair of strong arms are smoothing
a thin red coverlet so carefully
he must be expecting someone. The scene's
too fragmentary to construct a convincing story,

but he smoothes the cloth until
I imagine there's not a single wrinkle
on the scarlet spread blushing
the lamplight so that his arms glow
with the color of intimacy. Even

after I'm tired of watching
there's something all night to wake me:
a pigeon flapping toward the sill
like an awkward annunciation, someone singing
in the alley thirteen floors down

—the Ode to Joy?—curiosity
about the red room a floor below, empty now.
In the park, the lamps' circles shrink
along distant paths beneath intricate trees,
Fifth Avenue luminous in its Roman,

floodlit splendor, and there the hulk
of the Metropolitan, where the Neapolitan angels
must be suspended in darkness now,
their glazed silks dim,
though their tempera skin's so polished

even an exit sign would set them blazing.
I'm sleeping a little then thinking
of the single male angel, lithe and radiant,
wrapped only in a Baroque scrap
sculpted by impossible wind. Because

he's slightly built—real, somehow—
there's something shocking
in his nakedness, the svelte hips
barely brushed by drapery;
he's no sexless bearer of God's thoughts.

Divinity includes desire
—why else create a world
like this one, dawn fogging
the park in gold, the Moorish arches
of the Y one grand Italian Bethlehem

in which the minor figures wake
in anticipation of some unforeseen beginning.
Even the pigeons seem glazed
and expectant, fired to iridescence.
And on the twelfth floor

just the perfect feet and ankles
of the boy in the red-flushed room
are visible. I think he must be disappointed,
stirring a little, alone, and then
two other legs enter the rectangle of view,

moving toward his and twining with them,
one instep bending to stroke
the other's calf. They make me happy,
these four limbs in effortless conversation
on their snowy ground, the sheets

curling into the billows sculptors used once
to make the suspension of gravity
visible. It doesn't matter
that it isn't silk. I haven't much evidence
to construe what binds them,

but the narrative windows
will offer all morning the glad tidings
of union, comfort and joy,
though I will not stay to watch them.

Turtle, Swan

Because the road to our house
is a back road, meadowlands punctuated
by gravel quarry and lumberyard,
there are unexpected travelers
some nights on our way home from work.
Once, on the lawn of the Tool

and Die Company, a swan;
the word doesn't convey the shock
of the thing, white architecture
rippling like a pond's rain-pocked skin,
beak lifting to hiss at my approach.
Magisterial, set down in elegant authority,

he let us know exactly how close we might come.
After a week of long rains
that filled the marsh until it poured
across the road to make in low woods
a new heaven for toads,
a snapping turtle lumbered down the center

of the asphalt like an ambulatory helmet.
His long tail dragged, blunt head jutting out
of the lapidary prehistoric sleep of shell.
We'd have lifted him from the road
but thought he might bend his long neck back
to snap. I tried herding him; he rushed,

though we didn't think those blocky legs
could hurry—then ambled back
to the center of the road, a target

for kids who'd delight in the crush
of something slow with the look
of primeval invulnerability. He turned

the blunt spear point of his jaws,
puffing his undermouth like a bullfrog,
and snapped at your shoe,
vising a beakful of—thank God—
leather. You had to shake him loose. We left him
to his own devices, talked on the way home

of what must lead him to new marsh
or old home ground. The next day you saw,
one town over, remains of shell
in front of the little liquor store. I argued
it was too far from where we'd seen him,
too small to be his... though who could tell

what the day's heat might have taken
from his body. For days he became a stain,
a blotch that could have been merely
oil. I did not want to believe that
was what we saw alive in the firm center
of his authority and right

to walk the center of the road,
head up like a missionary moving certainly
into the country of his hopes.
In the movies in this small town
I stopped for popcorn while you went ahead
to claim seats. When I entered the cool dark

I saw straight couples everywhere,
no single silhouette who might be you.
I walked those two aisles too small
to lose anyone and thought of a book
I read in seventh grade, *Stranger than Science,*
in which a man simply walked away,

at a picnic, and was,
in the act of striding forward
to examine a flower, gone.

By the time the previews ended
I was nearly in tears—then realized
the head of one-half the couple in the first row

was only your leather jacket propped in the seat
that would be mine. I don't think I remember
anything of the first half of the movie.
I don't know what happened to the swan. I read
every week of some man's lover showing
the first symptoms, the night sweat

or casual flu, and then the wasting begins
and the disappearance a day at a time.
I don't know what happened to the swan;
I don't know if the stain on the street
was our turtle or some other. I don't know
where these things we meet and know briefly,

as well as we can or they will let us,
go. I only know that I do not want you
—you with your white and muscular wings
that rise and ripple beneath or above me,
your magnificent neck, eyes the deep mottled autumnal colors
of polished tortoise—I do not want you ever to die.

Homo Will Not Inherit

Downtown anywhere and between the roil
of bathhouse steam—up there the linens of joy
and shame must be laundered again and again,

all night—downtown anywhere
and between the column of feathering steam
unknotting itself thirty feet above the avenue's

shimmered azaleas of gasoline,
between the steam and the ruin
of the Cinema Paree (marquee advertising

its own milky vacancy, broken showcases sealed,
ticketbooth a hostage wrapped in tape
and black plastic, captive in this zone

of blackfronted bars and bookstores
where there's nothing to read
but longing's repetitive texts,

where desire's unpoliced, or nearly so)
someone's posted a xeroxed headshot
of Jesus: permed, blonde, blurred at the edges

as though photographed through a greasy lens,
and inked beside him, in marker strokes:
HOMO WILL NOT INHERIT. *Repent and be saved.*

I'll tell you what I'll inherit: the margins
which have always been mine, downtown after hours
when there's nothing left to buy,

the dreaming shops turned in on themselves,
seamless, intent on the perfection of display,
the bodegas and offices lined up, impenetrable:

edges no one wants, no one's watching. Though
the borders of this shadow-zone (mirror and dream
of the shattered streets around it) are chartered

by the police, and they are required,
some nights, to redefine them. But not now, at twilight,
permission's descending hour, early winter darkness

pillared by smoldering plumes. The public city's
ledgered and locked, but the secret city's boundless;
from which do these tumbling towers arise?

I'll tell you what I'll inherit: steam,
and the blinding symmetry of some towering man,
fifteen minutes of forgetfulness incarnate.

I've seen flame flicker around the edges of the body,
pentecostal, evidence of inhabitation.
And I have been possessed of the god myself,

I have been the temporary apparition
salving another, I have been his visitation, I say it
without arrogance, I have been an angel

for minutes at a time, and I have for hours
believed—without judgment, without condemnation—
that in each body, however obscured or recast,

is the divine body—common, habitable—
the way in a field of sunflowers
you can see every bloom's

the multiple expression
of a single shining idea,
which is the face hammered into joy.

I'll tell you what I'll inherit:
stupidity, erasure, exile
inside the chalked lines of the police,

who must resemble what they punish,
the exile you require of me,
you who's posted this invitation

to a heaven nobody wants.
You who must be patrolled,
who adore constraint, I'll tell you

what I'll inherit, not your pallid temple
but a real palace, the anticipated
and actual memory, the moment flooded

by skin and the knowledge of it,
the gesture and its description
—do I need to say it?—

the flesh *and* the word. And I'll tell you,
you who can't wait to abandon your body,
what you want me to, maybe something

like you've imagined, a dirty story:
Years ago, in the baths,
a man walked into the steam,

the gorgeous deep indigo of him gleaming,
solid tight flanks, the intricately ridged abdomen—
and after he invited me to his room,

nudging his key toward me,
as if perhaps I spoke another tongue
and required the plainest of gestures,

after we'd been, you understand,
worshipping a while in his church,
he said to me, *I'm going to punish your mouth.*

I can't tell you what that did to me.
My shame was redeemed then;
I won't need to burn in the afterlife.

It wasn't that he hurt me,
more than that: the spirit's transactions
are enacted now, here—no one needs

your eternity. This failing city's
radiant as any we'll ever know,
paved with oily rainbow, charred gates

jeweled with tags, swoops of letters
over letters, indecipherable as anything
written by desire. I'm not ashamed

to love Babylon's scrawl. How could I be?
It's written on my face as much as on
these walls. This city's inescapable,

gorgeous, and on fire. I have my kingdom.

David Trinidad

(1953 –

A native of Los Angeles, David Trinidad now lives and works in New York City. His poems have been included in dozens of anthologies and numerous magazines. There are nine published collections of his work. He currently teaches poetry at Rutgers University, where he directs the "Writers at Rutgers" series, and is a member of the core faculty in the MFA writing program at The New School.

Delphi

My parents first heard it
   from the school psychologist.
It stood out in my artwork
   like a cardboard kitchenette, a jump rope,
a doll. It seeped from my mouth

in stammered speech.
   It had to be stopped, so they sent me
to summer camps, to Little League, to Cub Scout
   meetings. But still it plagued me
like a tetanus shot. I cried helpless and they

gave me candy to get me through. Afterwards,
   the stain remained on my tongue, my teeth,
my lips—red like blood. It was not the sort of thing
   they could nip in the bud.
The neighborhood first heard it

from the radio, the television, the news.
   They read it on labels.
It disrupted each marriage like a woman's curse
   and clung to the landscape,
a pestilent cloud threatening

to infect every lung.
  I never chose my own clothes.
There was absolutely nothing I could do.
  Like this birthmark on my ankle,
it has always been there.

I first heard it from the playground.
  It flew fast as a football in the air and followed me
across the asphalt like a dirty word.
  In cul-de-sacs, the nosy bitch parted drapes
to taunt me with prophetic glares:

We shall stare at you, we shall always stare.
  It burned in my ear like gossip or parents quarrelling.
Later, I heard it whispered
  during lunch hours and in locker rooms.
I ran home from school every day, but it kept at me,

clawed at my window-screen like a hungry cat.
  I did not know they'd throw me out
like scandal sheets
  and cast me in bad shows.
I was blacklisted by the stars.

And they've been spreading the rumor ever since.

The Gift of Dionysus

As the flasks were passed, I sensed
his presence—intense, stirring.
I stared into the fire we had built
and huddled about as if bewitched,
fixed on an image of our god. Vague,
wavering, a shape slid towards me
like a leopard; his features appeared
clear—wild hair wreathed with grape
clusters, bearded face, bare chest,
leather sandal-straps that crisscrossed his

muscular calves. An arm prodded,
offered the spout I accepted, lifting
it to my lips, gently, like an open
mouth, which I kissed as I stretched
back. The wine tasted sweet, thick
as spit. The boy nearest me leaned
over and licked the juice that trickled
down my neck like a bear lapping sap
as it seeps in between the grooved
trunk of a tree. Above us, the tips
of cypresses shook in the wintry breeze
like black flames. Sparks drifted up
then dropped into the fringes of the
darkness. His hands slipped between and
separated my thighs. A scream. I opened
my eyes as several blurred women went
after a buck they'd spotted observing us
in the vibrating light. Bodies leapt
apart and darted off. I allowed myself
to be tugged, shoved through the woods—
stumbled down a slope, crossed a brook,
came to a clearing where they'd surrounded
and slain the creature. Two men held
it up; another stabbed at it, slit
its belly. Suddenly, I was seized from
behind and pushed forward, onto my knees,
my face pressed against the beast—sacred
the heart of his flesh, his heat. More
came, carrying torches. The carcass
was dragged away. Women smeared blood
across their breasts, laughed, snatched
pieces of meat, retreated to bushes.
The rest of us circled the blood-soaked
soil. Our chant grew frantic. I threw my head
back, spun about, flung my fists at the
full moon which looked upon us like
an approving eye. The high pines were
spinning. One by one, we dropped to the
damp grass. As I collapsed, I imagined
his cloak covering us—exquisite, with
vines of black grapes, snakes, and rams
sipping from a river which wound down
to our world, overflowing with wine.

Dream Creatures

The centaur showed us what strength was.
Although his hoof-prints were snowflake-shaped,
his heart was a star.
He took us to the glass castle,
into black forests, stamping
a path through the brier.
A centaur is sturdy,
rarely defeated.

Then the dwarf taught us about chance.
He swallowed our loose change and lit up.
We watched his eyeballs
spin as fast as a slot machine—
oranges and stars blurred black like
muddy watercolors—
slowing down past the hearts,
stopping at cherries.

Now a wizard exposes us
to evil: rain, the corrupt household.
He flaunts silk capes and
sequined stars, hearts. As he haunts us
at night, spreading his shadow,
the hexed lilies open
and close, in dream-moonlight,
like black umbrellas.

The Boy

Looking back,
I think that he must have been an angel.
We never spoke,
but one entire summer, every day,
he sat on the curb across the street.
I watched him: thin, his skin white,
his blond hair cut short.

Sometimes, right after swimming,
his bathing suit wet and tight,
he would sit and dry off in the sun.
I couldn't stop staring.

Then late one night,
toward the end of the summer,
he appeared in my room.
Perhaps that's why
I've always considered him
an angel: silent, innocent, pale
even in the dark.
He undressed
and pulled back the sheet,
slid next to me.
His fingers felt for my lips.

But perhaps I am not remembering
correctly.
Perhaps he never came
into my room that night.
Perhaps he never existed
and I invented him.
Or perhaps it was me, not blond
but dark, who sat all summer
on that sunny corner: seventeen
and struggling to outlast
my own restlessness.

Pavane

The two silhouettes separate
from the shadows, emerge
as distinct figures
poised some distance apart.
They face one another
at the edge of the lake.
A star briefly skims across it,
unsettling the surface
like a small white stone.

Gently, the breeze bends
the grass into the blue water.
One by one, clouds appear
and demand attention,
a procession of familiar gestures—
memories mounting.
There will be grief
There will be a great loss
the woods whisper.
And because it is cold,
because it is dark,
the figures take the necessary steps.
They cling
to each other
and silently,
in defiance,
dance.

Love Poem

At 4:30 A.M., I wake up
from a nightmare, bump
through the dark apartment
to pee, then sit and smoke
a cigarette in the living
room. When I get back
in bed, Ira wakes up
and says: "You're a sweet
man, do you know that?"
I tell him I've been having
bad dreams. I'm lying on
my back; he tells me to roll
on my side. As I do, he presses
against me from behind and
wraps his arm around my chest.
"You're safe now," he whispers
into my neck. "Go back to sleep.
You won't have any more bad dreams."

Gavin Geoffrey Dillard

(1954 –

Playwright, songwriter, artist, photographer, Gavin Dillard is the author of seven collections of poetry, two anthologies, and his Hollywood memoirs. In the '70s and '80s, his regular in-the-buff poetry readings won him the moniker of "The Naked Poet." A native of Appalachia, he currently resides with a menagerie of cats on the foggy cliffs of Northern California.

The Lure

The lure is too strong
I want to be rich for him
I want to be famous for him,
really famous
I want him to want me for
all the wrong reasons,
for any reason
I want him to want me
until, satisfied, he
forgets all want for
anyone else,
the way that I was
never able to do.

Jeske

He could work in any
Polish factory, his
long smooth and
shining white flesh

Any Hungarian sweatshop
his long-dangling balls

sweating, like eggs in a
wet sock banging between
those treetrunk legs

And I, a little peasant
girl might see him one
day and, knowing that he
would never bring me
wealth

Marry him anyway and have
his children, just
for the dank and dreamy
factory smell

Beneath his arms, in
his socks and boxer
shorts, every day when he
comes home from work.

Yellow Snow

Yellow snow
wherever he goes,
it's all that coffee
he says, but knows
it's more than that,
it's something genetic,
he's marking his trail
alchemic, hermetic,
he's writing in runes
while I collect bones
and follow behind
eating yellow snow cones.

Drinking Trebor's Pee

To drink Trebor's pee
sweetened, with lemon over ice
would be a bastardization of the
Truth; one
drinks Trebor's pee, like one
swallows Trebor's semen, hot and
directly from the fount—
or at least within minutes from a
favored mug or goblet.

I consume Trebor's pee the way I
consume Trebor's words, without
question or editing of my own
conceits; who
am I to challenge the visceral ejacu
lations of so worthy and proud a
beast?
I seduce; I consume.
I succumb; I am consumed.

Love is neither easy nor attractive,
wholesome nor sane;
when Trebor speaks, worlds are rent
askew, hearts pried from their ossi
fied tombs; when
Trebor speaks my gonads quiver, my
scrotum tightens and my anus
convulses with the revelations of a
burgeoning dawn.

Who am I to challenge this mystic-
eyed mongrel; I
set out my bowls, plates, and watch the
varmint pick and choose from my
table—
if I am lucky he naps on my sofa be
fore wandering back to his sacred
wood; if I am
lucky he stops to feed me from his
trove of used poems and found
objects; if I am truly

lucky he does not bite me but re
sponds to my caress with a
sigh or a low growl,

and I know that I have fed Trebor some
thing he can use,
that my offerings have been
accepted—

and this is more than enough for
one small lifetime.

It's Been a Long Time Since I've Lived with a Straight Boy

Billy's been here a week and everything
smells of him.
Strong smells. Intense, aggressive
smells.
Not just the reek of Old Spice all over the
bathroom sink, lining the tub,
but the construction sites in their
entirety, big men, steel-backed men,
burly black men and truckloads of
dusty Mexicans;
a lockerroom hanging from his bedroom
walls, oozing from blankets and
pillows—the small bathroom
rug that wafts entirely of
rank socks, as if some elixir had spilt
out of his boots.
His towel, two days fresh, has a
life of its own, matted with
hairs, exuding pheromones—
what are these little gray balls in the
bathtub drain?

In the kitchen I boil pungent Chinese
herbs, burn Tibetan incense and
pour elegant teas;
in my bedroom, the tastes of

sperm always linger, some
lotion or another, the
sour breath of latex.

Can he smell me for what I am?
Oh not just the Royal Copenhagen I wear to
remind me of Granddad,
but the urine I've consumed,
the semen I have bathed in,
the feces that have permeated my
pubic rags, the smoke, the
nitrates; the fine dining in my
brain, the elegant hotels,
the liqueurs, the wines that
critics covet?

Here he is now after pouring
concrete all day, blue collar to the
neck with mud and grease
to boot;
moments from now his steam will
blast these aromas thru curtain thru
doors, into towels and pores,
he'll come clean, but his imprint will
ever remain, in the head of
the air, in the strains, in my
hair—
it hardly seems fair,
but certainly I will become accustomed.

Courting Rodney

Rodney is an extraordinarily beauteous young man of thirty.
When he was twenty, the wrong dosage administered in a
hospital somewhere crippled him and zapped his
nerves. His back is crooked, his hands gnarled with
palsy, and his legs, thick and muscular beneath
loose-fitting shorts, curl in and shake from
his body's own weight.

He cannot speak, but carries around a portable
computer on which he is capable of rapidly
punching out responses to queries—he
is not shy about using this device. I
was not introduced to the lad, but
hastily offered that he
share my table.

He had just returned from a hospital up in Canada that
he hoped would be able to cauterize the glands which
salivate a continual stream down his chin; they
put him on another medication (which
appeared to not work very well). I
desired to offer my hair and my
lips to keep him dry.

I do not know of his sex life, before or after the
"accident" when he was twenty; I would love to
watch his paralysis respond to an orgasm (if he
can have such). Rodney smiled and cavorted with
the employees of the cafe, who all knew and
loved him; yes, someone answered me, he is
always this effulgent—I wanted to
ask of his romantic proclivities,
but did not.

Perhaps he was just being shy with a stranger, or
maybe he presumed that I would not be inspired by a
case such as his; I desired to inform him that I
am a cripple too, that my disease is inside and
needs a patient hand and a steady heart. But I
merely watched him bounce out with his to-go
burritos and the small shoulder purse in
which he carries both computer and a
book of paper towels.

Next time lunch will be on me, I will feed him his
meal and wipe the napkins across his proud chin and
contorting lips; when we are done we will lie
together, trembling with the spasms of spent
passion, sharing secrets of how the world has
damaged us, and how two spirits can soar
above this troubled, palsied terra.

Orange Kitty Bleeding

I killed the old orange cat this evening.
After chasing him for three months, I
crawled up on the roof after him;
right between the eyes from not more than
five feet away where he had Bagheera
treed up the great live oak.
Orange Kitty fell and I blasted him four
more times as he jerked on the ground
below us.
Bagheera came down from his high branch;
and after, I brought out Marlene, Tao and
Quan Yin to show them that the reign of
terror had ended.
But as he lay there with his fur blowing
gently in the oncoming storm, I had the
strongest urge to take his bloody form into
my arms, smooth his once-beautiful pelt and
tell him that it will all be
all right.

I miss all my old lovers, wherever they
lay bleeding beneath the grass, I would
take them all once again in my arms and
tell them that it is not that bad, that
it will all be all right;
death after all seems so unreachable to
the living, so temporary as though it
were but a mistake, a dream that will
fade back into the reality of the
sunny morn.

But I didn't touch the orange cat, he
was covered with blood and had been
sick, wild and unreachable as it was.
Instead, I thought of Vince Romano,
James Parcell, Steven Buker, Frank
Drummond, Jimmy Barron, Victor Lopez,
Bobby Consolmagno and however many
more;
warm warm hearts that had once
beat against my own, now cold lying

somewhere in the shadow of what had
been life, their fur now matted and
soiled.

The cats avenged, we came back into
the house just as the storm was blowing
in from the west.
I thought of Orange Kitty, of covering him
with newspapers or old clothes lest he
get cold and drenched where I had
left him among the periwinkle.
Instead I removed the bullets from the
remaining cartridge and set the twenty-
two across a pile of fresh-folded
linens, to be returned to the
neighbors in the morning.

The rain began spattering like
gunshot across the fiberglass back
porch roof;
my dinner was still warm.

Smoke Rings

Taylor and I, this evening,
cleared a large faerie/fire
ring in the upper pasture,
marking carefully with an old
nylon rope radius where the
stones will soon be placed,
and again notching a second
circle where lombardy poplars
are to be planted. We
burned grasses and debris from
trees surrounding, warming our
penes against the funnel of
flame, which lapped against
the overcast sky until at last
the semen drenched us to the
bone.

Pagan rituals left us brimming
with energy, the cats following
us back wild-eyed to the
house where beer, wine and
olives saturated our elated
senses.

Sated now, the rains are
steady and calming, our
flame extinguished but the
smoke in our eyes must never
clear.

This at last makes sense, two
old witches who have reunited
not for lust nor for love nor
money, but to rekindle a
flame of tradition that has
bound us for ages to the
same wooden stake, if only
to be burned again.

Tomales Point

We sat on Tomales Point,
his lips were dry and cracked inside my own;
I could taste what we had had for lunch some
three hours before.

We had hiked to this precipice,
my body stank of tea and musk, and brine
dripped down my arms onto his;
he smelled of coffee and citrus.

An ex Jesuit, he spoke of his monastic
life and current wiccan studies while I
strew seeds of opium poppies, datura, nicotina and
Siberian motherwort upon the wild, mist-
dampened terrain.

Dinner that nite was casual and
makeshift, I sucked on his tits until I could
taste the ale he was drinking;
we never unbuttoned our pants.

Love is tame after forty, but it is
no less splendid;
out on the bluffs, the herds of tule elk were
completely hornless, that had boasted such
awesome racks mere weeks before.

On the trail, a boy of no more than
five gleamed and boasted of the single
antler he had found in the bush.

Goatboy

Goatboy thinks he's Pan
and maybe he is,
who am I to say
strange passion, this!
What recourse have I
when horns do sprout,
but to watch the child grow stout
and goat about.

Who am I to criticize
the raptures of youth,
make angels of devils
or decry goatly truths?
Goatboy thinks he's Pan
and well he may be,
he'll find no reprimand
from an old satyr like me.

The Wife of Lot

Were God to take me by the hand
to my bed reserved, The Promised Land,
would he find me, wistful, gazing back
toward smoking hills and ocean black,

Mournful of this world gone sour,
longing in that judgment hour
for one last breath of clover sweet,
a deft embrace, a swollen teat,

The eyes of lovers, insecure,
the voice of sorrow, wrath, allure,
temptation like a treasured wine
which seeps from grapes yet on the vine?

I think, all things considered be,
the Lord might have to pardon me,
that whilst that final second tolls
and angels harvest all good souls,

That I, as hearts are laid to waste,
may linger for one final taste.

Epitaph:

*When last I lie
to rest my head
let it not be said
I missed a bed.*

Michael Gregg Michaud

(1955 –

Michael Gregg Michaud was born in a potato field in Readfield, Maine, and currently lives in the killing fields of Los Angeles, just seven miles from Keanu Reeves. His work has been widely published and anthologized, and he once stole, and continues to wear, a pair of Matt Dillon's sneakers. He works with Tippi Hedren at her Shambala big cat preserve.

The Night Joe Dallesandro Puked On Me

Joe stood unsteadily in the shower
leaning back away from the hot water.
Wash yourself, I said.
But he swayed as the water splashed
at his feet.
I stripped and climbed in,
pushing him into the steaming spray.
He arched his back
and looked up sleepily into my eyes,
What're you doin'?
Trying to wash you, I said,
soaping his chest, his soft nipples
and hard belly.
Why? I'm not a baby, he mumbled.
You stink, I said as I gently wiped
the festering tracks in his left arm,
then lathered between his legs,
cupping his balls,
and taking his cock in my sudsy hands.
I'm sick, he exclaimed.
His body became rigid and he puked,
hitting me in the chest with a hot
lumpy spray of vodka and the blueberry cake
I had hand fed him earlier.
The vomit ran down my legs as he choked up more
and I reached out to pull him against me.

He puked streams over my shoulder
and down my back.
It ran hot in the crack of my ass.
I held him tight as he retched,
feeling his body convulse
and his stomach muscles clench
against my belly.
As he coughed up more, I felt a tingling
and my erection popped up hard between us.
I turned him around and away from the hot water
and lowered him into the tub.
Without washing myself,
I grabbed my cock covered with his puke
and pumped for just a moment before
I came against the shower door
and across his legs at my feet.
Joe looked up slowly, vomit slimed across his chest,
and with a crooked smile mumbled,
that was the best blueberry cake
I ever had.

Heartthrob

I don't look at movie magazines or write
silly fan letters, and I refuse to make a
fool of myself, but I do love Keanu Reeves.
The first time I saw him I was sitting in
a movie theatre on La Brea Avenue catching
a matinee. I watched him walk in. Alone.
Wearing a jean jacket and baseball hat.
I'm sure I caught his eye. After the movie,
I followed him to the bathroom where he
stood at the urinal, but before I could
talk to him, eleven other guys burst through
the door pushing me against the sinks.
I chipped a front tooth and cut my lip.
The second time I saw Keanu Reeves I was
walking down Rose Avenue in Venice while
they were filming a scene from *Speed*.

As I carefully stepped over electrical cords
along the sidewalk, he walked right
past me wearing a brown T-shirt, jeans
and boots, carrying a styrofoam coffee cup.
I'm sure he smiled. I think he remembered me
from the bathroom. The third time I saw Keanu
Reeves I was having coffee at The Living Room
on La Brea Avenue. He ordered a cappuccino and
a chocolate chip cookie, then went upstairs,
two steps at a time, to play pool. I went up
to watch, but he didn't notice me because
he was concentrating on his game. I bought him
another cappuccino but I spilled it on the floor
and it splashed on his helmet. The fourth
time I saw Keanu Reeves, he strode into MAXX
bar, ordered a bottle of beer, stood at the bar
to drink it, and looked around the crowded room.
I waved. I'm sure he saw me. Then he left. The
fifth time I saw Keanu Reeves, he almost ran
over me in the crosswalk at Sunset and Laurel.
His 1972 Norton 850 Commando motorcycle missed
me by inches. I'm sure he smiled. I think he
remembered me from MAXX.

The Night Keanu Reeves Kicked Me In the Face

About the time I knew I was in trouble
I was crawling on all fours
in a crowded nightclub
trying to get under Keanu Reeves' table.
He had broken his ankle a few weeks before
in a motorcycle accident
and his foot was still in a cast.
What on earth are you doing, a woman asked me.
I dropped a contact, I fumbled.
But you're wearing glasses.
It wasn't mine, I said
as I quickly crept to his table.
I saw his foot, his naked toes

just inches from my nose once I was
under the tablecloth.
I moved a little closer, my heart pounding,
as I strained to see in the dim light
and struggled to detect his odor.
His toes were long and callused,
his big toe flat and wide,
the little pinkie twisted inward.
His dirty nails were longish
and curled ever so slightly
down around the end of each digit.
I moved so close I could smell
the dryness, the staleness of his foot.
I wanted to take each dusty little kicker
slowly into my mouth,
let my tongue roll between each gummy bear,
flick each nail,
and suck like a nursing babe,
licking under and around,
pinching each one hard between my teeth,
playing with the wonky, wiry hairs
on his toe knuckles,
kissing sweetly, smooth and delicious,
brown between my lips.
But then he moved his toes,
slightly stretching toward me,
pointing each, one at a time at my nose
just barely an inch away.
And then moved his foot abruptly,
slamming the cast against my left cheekbone,
sending my glasses clattering to the floor,
drawing blood from my nose
with his razor nails,
painfully sweet as a first kiss,
and I was in heaven.

How To Be a Gay Literary Icon

Say you knew Tennessee Williams.
Say you slept with him.
He's dead, who'll know?
Enter your latest book
in the annual Lambda Literary Awards
and vote for yourself.
Be sullen.
Be fat with a receding hairline
a 44 inch waist
and a mother complex.
Frequent hustler bars.
Be photographed with Sandra Bernhard, Madonna,
or Jeff Stryker.
Dedicate your books to dead people
or your analyst.
Be photographed for your book jacket
tightly clutching a pet cat.
It doesn't need to be yours.
Pretend to know Camille Paglia.
Accept every party invitation
but never go.
Tell engaging anecdotes
about radical writer groups in the 1960s
and imply you were there.
Mope.
Heckle at Republican rallies
but only when covered by network news.
Have a handsome young boyfriend,
preferably a college gymnast.
Pay him if you have to.
If you pay him,
call him your research assistant.
Cough a lot.
Smile sadly when you talk about Stonewall.
Fill your home with autographed books
but never read them.
Pay your friends to be shills at your readings
and tell them to laugh very loudly.
Cue them with a telling nod.
Apply for grants you will never receive
and blame it on homophobia.

Come from a broken home.
Speak in hushed tones and wear glasses.
Tell each young male fan he, too, can write,
with the proper instruction.
Give him your phone number.
Talk about "gay sensibility"
and sound like you know what it means.
Affect an accent.
Any accent will do.
Claim to be an abused child.
Be co-dependent
and never politically correct.
Have compulsive addictions to drugs,
alcohol, and/or sex.
Be in recovery.
Don't quit your day job.

Michael Hathaway

(1961 –

Michael Hathaway works for an organization that serves people with mental disabilities. He edits and publishes Chiron Review, *a literary magazine he founded in 1982 with his mother, Jane. He lives in St John, Kansas, with his best friend, Rusty, and twelve cats.*

me & ratboy run the gamut of literary lovers

sometimes we're jack & neal,
poking & challenging each others'
minds & histories,
entire belief systems
in motel rooms & cars
with no destinations

drunken thoughts & words
roll across the black manuscript
of strange city night skies

we move & run
as if our lives depend upon it

sometimes we are auden & kallman
and i hate him for being young.
i hate him for being in love
with the whole world.
i hate the whole world
for being in love with him.

sometimes i am
ginsberg & williams
& he is nameless tasty chicken,
i beg him to let me
help every inch
of his long brown body
into heaven

but he is most at ease
when we are Beavis & Butthead,
stuck in small Kansas towns
with no money,
punching each other,
biting each other,
exploring the taste of blood,
the art of pain,
creating fat purple bruises
on the canvas of our bodies.

i'm not a punching bag but...

he is stronger than me
and likes to hit

it is an art.
his eyes dilate,
his face gets a hard mean look,
he doubles his fist and swings wide,
brown biceps bulge

i like it,
the way it jars my whole being
that thud on my arm
or leg, or back, once in the eye
(you really do see stars)

the sheer male power behind the punch.
i never had that power,
it always mystifies, eludes me.

i like seeing it, feeling it,
understanding it

i take his touch, his skin
any way he offers it.

what would Grandma think?

every Saturday, Ratboy and I jump into the car,
with a case of Keystone Light
and a bottle of Southern Comfort
and hit the highway
with no particular destination.

we find a town we think might be groovy,
rent a motel room and commence to enjoy
the finer things in life:

Diet Coke mixed lightly with
lots of Southern Comfort,
beer chasers, delivered pizza,
Beavis & Butthead on MTV,

wrestling and fighting during commercials,
slamming each others' heads against the walls,
power pillow fights, broken lamps,
busted ribs, jammed fingers, fistfuls of hair,
teeth marks from head to toe,
beer fights which saturate our clothes,
back flips from one bed to another...

3 a.m. finds us exhausted, lying there,
our brains floating pleasantly
in pools of alcohol.

my eyes scope the room:
i spy the nightstand covered with beer cans
and bottles of booze.

Grandma's sweet face flashes before my eyes,
and her stern words:
"never set anything on top of a Bible."

i respectfully and carefully
remove all the beer cans
and the fifth of Southern Comfort
off the Gideon Bible,
pretty sure Grandma is smiling
down from heaven in approval.

the club

when Ratboy ran off with the carnival last May,
it hit me hard.

i was inundated with heartbroken bimbos
ringing my doorbell: where is he?!?
when is he coming home?!?

the first one cried on my shoulder,
I tried to comfort her, said,
"you know he is a wild free spirit,
no one can hold him. that's partly
why we love him, why we have to
let him go."
She said, "i know you miss him too."
She left, tears glistening down her cheeks.

the second said sarcastically,
"do *you* know where he is?
he tells *you* everything..."
i said, "yeah i know. he's flown head first
into the future embracing his destiny
with a great big bear hug
and there ain't nothin' you or I
or anyone else can do to stop him."

the third was hysterical,
a brain-dead bug-eyed girl,
"Where is he? Where is he? I've been
crying for three days!!!"

I sneered,
"Join the club, bitch"
and slammed the door.

cinnamon man

the last time i saw tracy
it was spring & all six feet of him
was sprawled in a pear tree,
his brown cinnamon form
barely clothed in snug denim cutoffs.
he was smoking weed,
mutilating pear blossoms,
showering himself & me
with the shredded white remains.
from the ground i asked him
to climb down
so he could get a secret from me.
he howled like a moon-crazed werewolf,
said he was real busy
at the moment.
i knew that.
but it didn't stop my wanting him.
it didn't stop my needing
his wicked knockabout love.
it didn't stop me from nibbling
the mangled blossoms
off his dangling cinnamon feet.

Trebor

(1962 –

The author of five chapbooks of poetry and co-editor of a recent anthology of gay and lesbian poetry and fiction, Trebor is widely anthologized and a regular at poetry events in both San Francisco and Los Angeles. He currently lives in Hollywood—en route to Mexico—where he is writing a novel and a screenplay.

We Started out Janitors

and ended up fuckbuddies
He used to mop the floors without a word
while I vacuumed couches and dusted tables

I figured he didn't speak English
We both figured the other was straight
We started out janitors
now I clean his asshole with my tongue

It was a restaurant
we both started stealing food from the fridge
big sausages and blocks of cheese
We started laughing one day when a cube of butter
dropped out of his pants as we were locking up to leave
We laughed so fucking hard
and then he said "I hate this job—
let's take everything and not come back tomorrow"
We started out janitors   now we're thieves

He said his boyfriend liked pastries as he bagged 3 dozen blintzes
I said I'm queer too
He said the only thing he liked more than food was sex
I said you wanna fuck?
He turned and forced his tongue in my mouth hard
We tore at each other's clothes
we both had big ugly dicks
that we treated like food

We started out janitors
and now we were sucking cock on the kitchen floor
He fucked me as I held the back of a chair
and I came onto his mopped floor
We laughed some more and took all the food

We both showed up the next day
I guess to find each other
took everything and came back
they didn't fire us   they didn't even notice
We stayed working there for 2 more months
fucking like crazy and cleaning less and less
We started out janitors
now we're fucking-connoisseurs in a high-class restaurant

We both got fired in the end
for doing a lousy job
But what did they know?
          (our asses spit-shined!)
We started out janitors
now we're unemployed fuckbuddies with something better to do

Hustler

He had a bank card for a cock
He'd insert it into horny old men with money
he knew all the right buttons to push
and he'd thrust his beautiful credit in
over and over again
pumping his payback
while the machine groaned
and made those chirping sounds
like a bird
$20 for every thrust
bang bang bang
and the twenties would pop out like blackheads
bang bang bang
like a slot machine

He was a one-organed bandit
And he laughed when he saw the oranges
and the apples
line up in rows in the old man's eyes

Jesus Christ, St. Sebastian, Etc., Etc.

Your body
        is a crucifixion
    and your arms look best that way
the hair in your armpits   finally flowing
            like lamenting   music

that bent rib you have is the spear in your side
        O, your tits
are like the madonna's tearful eyes
            round and soft   powerless and tender

The bold hairiness of your legs   is saying quite plainly
I WALKED THIS MOUNTAIN
I AM WILLING TO BE HERE
            your feet are endurance
and   of course   sorrow

The firm softness of your buttocks
    is pressed   lightly
        against the hard wood
                like how it presses against me
I want to apologize to its innocence

Your back is finally stretched
            lightened of burden
your hands are finally open and empty   nailed into submission
having dropped   what they held   like sleep
            no more to do, to shape

Your cock   elegantly erect
            curves like a finger   motioning forward
            into the darkness and thickness

                        of its surrounding blooming–african–violets
the hair on your inner thighs   like a   thin stand   of pines
along a tundric peninsula   wide   and breathtaking   as wilderness

Your face is asleep   or peacefully dead
                    with a faint smile
the contrast of your dark hair   and pale olive skin
is as   assertively aesthetic
            as   calligraphy on white paper

Crown of thorns
                    ——bite me
this cup will not pass
and I stand in the rain of your blood

It is the picadores then
and your heart is plunged full of swords
the immaculate heart of Mary
Sorrowful and Glorious
Sweet Homosexual Junkie

Reginald Shepherd

(1963 –

Reginald Shepherd grew up in the Bronx, attended a vast assortment of colleges and universities, and now lives in Chicago. He has three books published by the University of Pittsburgh Press, is an assistant professor of English at Northern Illinois University, and collects all CD versions of Strauss and Wagner operas.

Eros in his Striped Blue Shirt

and green plaid shorts goes strolling
through Juneau Park at eight o'clock
with only a hooded yellow windbreaker
for protection, trawling the bushes after work

while tugboats crawl the darkening freshwater
outlook. Mist coming in not even from a sea, rain
later in the evening from Lake Michigan, a promise
like *wait till your father gets home.* The air

is full of fog and botched seductions, reluctance
of early summer to arrive. It's fifty-five degrees
in June, the bodies can barely be made out
leaning on picnic tables under trees or

set sentinel like statues along the paths (the founder
corrodes quietly on his pedestal, inscription
effaced under **FAGGOTS GO HOME**). Lips
touched to a public fountain for a passerby

shape clouded breath into a *who-goes-there?*, into a
friend-or-foe?, eyes catching eyes like hooks
cast in a shallow tide. Night pouring in like water
into a lock, the rusted freighter lowered level

to level, banks of the cement canal
on either side, but miles from any dock.

Johnny Minotaur

This morning we can be kind to one another.
A trophy carried through the labyrinth
in the arms of a blind minotaur, you're wholly occupied
by pastimes of invisibility. *Enchanted,* I said once

(you smirked), taking the hand of difference, taken in
by what the retina takes in. Sullen boy, sight
sullies you; it's made you what you are. I prefer
to watch you sleep, your face adorned by lack,

your person sacrificed to first light slatted
through matte blinds. I'm not ready to give that up
just yet, the giving everything for what
the eye can see, for nothing, not for free;

I'm partial to the part of light that scribbles
on your cheek. (Your sleep finds me stealing kisses
from particulars, sight unseen: a parcel of you
you can't keep I'll carry from your room, untouched

by human hands.) The men you've rejected
will be in the bushes tonight, searching for a shadow
that looks like you. Sing them a lullaby to lead them out
with your amazing voice, but don't wake up.

A Muse

He winds through the party like wind, one of the just
who live alone in black and white, bewildered

by the eden of his body. *(You, you talk like winter
rain.)* He's the meaning of almost-morning walking home

at five a.m., the difference a night makes
turning over into day, simple birds staking claims

on no sleep. Whatever they call those particular birds.
He's the age of sensibility at seventeen, he isn't worth

the time of afternoon it takes to write this down.
He's the friend that lightning makes, raking

the naked tree, thunder that waits for weeks to arrive;
he's the certainty of torrents in September, harvest time

and powerlines down for miles. He doesn't even know
his name. In his body he's one with air, white as a sky

rinsed with rain. It's cold there, it's hard to breathe,
and drowning is somewhere to be after a month of drought.

Black is the Color of my True Love's Hair

In the painting by Guido Reni of Saint Sebastian
in the Palazzo Rosso, which reproduction makes available
to those who travel only on the page, the saint to be
(he's not yet assumed by artifice, encumbered

with perfections) endures continual martyrdom
with a visual sigh, gazing almost directly upward
as if to ask *What now my love,* or hum a chorus of
Is that all there is, the body always some song

or another. The eye tramping the simulacrum
of a surface hands have touched can't help but note
how lush the uncorrupted flesh appears: the curve, for one
example, of the waist (narrowest circuit of the boy),

just beneath the instance of an arrow's entrance, or
the shadow just above the tangled loin-cloth that is surely
pubic hair. One grasps that sainthood is an attribute of youth,
the *wondrous fair*, as in old ballads: they always end.

The boy in the Eagle Discount Supermarket,
for another, an apparition in a backwards baseball cap
appraising cuts of meat in artificial light,
deciding what he can afford

to buy, how much each cut costs. *I love the ground
on where he stands.* His face? Unverifiable.

Timothy Liu

(1965 –

Born and raised in California, Timothy Liu, a teacher and lecturer, has been widely published in reviews and periodicals. There are four published books of his verse, and his archives have just been acquired by the New York Public Library. Liu currently lives with the painter Christopher Arabadjis in Hoboken, New Jersey, and is an Assistant Professor at William Paterson University.

The Size of It

I knew the length of an average penis
      was five to seven inches, a fact
I learned upstairs in the stacks marked 610
      or HQ, not down in the basement
where I knelt behind a toilet stall, waiting
      for eight-and-a-half inches or more
to fill my mouth with a deeper truth. The heart
      grows smaller, like a cut rose drying
in the sun. Back then I was only fourteen,
      with four-and-three-quarters inches
at full erection. I began equating
      Asian with inadequate, unable
to compete with others in the locker room
      after an icy swim (a shriveled
bud between my fingers as I tried to shake
      some semblance of life back into it).
Three times a day, I jacked off faithfully, yet
      nothing would enlarge my future, not
ads for vacuum pumps, nor ancient herbs. Other
      men had to compensate, one billion
Chinese measured against what? Some said my cock
      had a classical shape, and I longed
for the ruins of Greece. Others took it up
      the ass, reassuring in their way,
yet nothing helped me much on my knees at night
      praying one more inch would make me whole.

Reading Whitman in a Toilet Stall

A security-man who stood, arms crossed, outside
the men's room (making sure that no one lingered)
met my eyes with the same dispassionate gaze as
a woman inside, kneeling to clean the toilets.

The faintly buzzing flicker of fluorescent light
erased the contours of a place where strangers
openly parade their sex. Efficient, silent,
all ammonia and rubber gloves, she was in and

out of there in minutes, taking no notice
of the pocket Whitman that I leafed my way through
before the others arrived. *In paths untrodden, /
In the growth by margins of pondwaters, / Escaped*

from the light that exhibits itself—how those words
came flooding back to me while men began to take
their seats, glory holes the size of silver dollars
in the farthest stall where no adolescent went

unnoticed. O daguerreotyped Walt, your collar
unbuttoned, hat lopsided, hand on hip, your sex
never evading our view! how we are confined
by steel partitions, dates and initials carved

into the latest coat of paint, an old car key
the implement of our secret desires. *Wanted:
uncut men with lots of cheese. No fats. No femmes.
Under twenty a real plus.* How each of us must

learn to decipher the erotic hieroglyphs
of our age, prayers on squares of one-ply paper
flushed daily down the john where women have knelt
in silence, where men with folded arms stand guard

while we go about our task, our tongues made holy
by licking each other's asshole clean, shock of sperm
warm in our mouths, white against the clothes we wear
as we walk out of our secrets into the world.

The Prodigal Son Writes Home

I want to tell you how he eats my ass
even in public places, Father dear,
the elastic round my waist his finger hooks
as it eases down my crack (no classified
ad our local paper would run, I'm afraid,
        but that's just as well).
We met in a bar that's gay one night a week—
teenage boys in cages, men on the floor,
but that's not what you want to hear, is it?
How he noses into my cheeks on callused knees,
lip-synching to the rage of techno-pop,
        that ecstasy of spit.

   ~

He's after me to shit into his hands.
What should I say? (I told him I'm afraid
he'd only smear it across my wide-eyed face,
hard as it is to tell you this.) How plans
have gone awry is more than apparent here—
        this sty he calls a home
tender as a mattress filled with our breath,
our sex unsafe. *Oh stay with me,* he croons,
my eyes clenched shut, head trying not to flinch
as he makes the sign of the cross on my chest
with a stream of steaming piss, asking me
        if we were born for this.

Mark Wunderlich

(1968 –

Mark Wunderlich grew up in rural Wisconsin. His work has been widely published and anthologized. His first book will be published by the University of Massachusetts Press in 1999. He has served as the director of the University of Arizona Poetry Center, and is currently a Wallace Stegner Fellow in poetry at Stanford University. He lives in San Francisco and Los Angeles.

Given in Person Only

Tompkins Square Park's a mess of shopping carts
overflowing with what's been cast off,
and pierced and tattooed punks affecting poses
soon grown into, arms speckling with tracks,
so when a girl extends a blue-nailed hand
I press to her palm the dollar she requests,

not because it will do her, or me a bit
of good, but because today I am willing
to give myself to anyone, should they ask.
I've just come back from the clinic,
its waiting room a jumble of second-hand plaid
where Lupita drew blood from a forearm's vein

she called *the kind she likes to see.*
Before her on the gun-metal desk
was the blueprint questionnaire mapping
my sexual history, the penciled dots
a constellation of what I wanted and what
I got. I know I've spent too much time

leaning against walls in bars, chewing ice
from an overpriced drink while shielding an ear
from some techno beat, the bass vibration
in the rib-cage the sound desire makes.
There have been back rooms where
I didn't know to whom the hands belonged

or how many, pure surrender. Then
there were the ones *with* names—
the man who bicycled through the snow,
stood in my living room and cried,
our bodies laboring to extinguish
some common flame, or the one

whose shirts still hang in my closet, limp torsos
washed out with use. I don't regret
the hunger that drove me to dark rooms,
stairwells, steam rooms or beaches,
park benches, parked cars, locker rooms
or clubs—locations that give shape

to my notion that sex is like faith—
at its center, it is always the same, unwavering.
I'll not apologize for the want and urge,
veiled in daylight as a curtain hides a stage,
no matter what Lupita will have for me
when she splits open her envelope's

folded white wings. In Chelsea the boys skate,
shirtless in late summer, brown thighs
and unflinching faces rolling by like gods.
It's muggy again, the way Manhattan
always seems in my dreams, and above
the water towers and angled roofs, the sun

insists on disrobing through the clouds.
I'll remake myself once again, shed
rapture and sweet release, and replace it
with something equally consummate and strange.
So let the city do as it must and break us down
to dust and skeletons. I'm just beginning.

The Trick

I made love with a man—hugely muscled, tan—the body
I've always wished for myself. He kept pulling my arms
up over my head, pinning them there, pressing me down

with his substantial weight, grinding into me roughly,
but then asked, begged, in a whisper of such sweetness,
Please kiss me. Earlier that evening, he told me

he'd watched a program about lions, admired
how they took their prey—menacing the herds at the water hole
before choosing the misfit, the broken one.

What surprised him was the wildebeests' calm
after the calf had been downed, how they returned to their grazing
with a dumb switching of tails. Nearby the lions looked up

from their meal, eyed the hopping storks and vultures,
before burying their faces, again, in the bloody ribs.
As a teenager, I wished to be consumed,

to be pressed into oblivion by a big forceful man.
It never happened. Instead I denied myself nourishment—
each un-filled plate staring back satisfied me, deprivation

reduced to a kind of bliss I could lie down in
where I remained unmoved, untouched.
Early on I was taught that the body was a cage,

that illness was a battle fought with chaos,
the viruses themselves unnatural; that sex lived
in some pastel chamber that gave way to infants,

first cousins, the handing down of names.
No one ever mentioned being taken in the dark,
or wanting to be broken open, pushed beyond words,

tongue thickening in another human mouth,
or how a person could be humiliated and like it.
To my surprise, I found myself struggling under this man,

pushing my chest up against his chest, arms straining
against the bed, until some younger, hungrier
version of myself lay back on top of me and took it—

the heaving back, the beard, the teeth at the throat.

Justin Chin

(1969 –

Justin Chin was born in Malaysia and raised in Singapore. A writer and a performance artist, he now resides in San Francisco. His first two collections of writings have just been released from Manic D Press, and from St Martin's.

Bergamot

In the beauty shop, the saleswoman dabs
a touch of bergamot to my right wrist;
I grind the spot staining
my thin skin and vulgar veins
stretched across my carpus to my left
wrist; the friction
spreads the scent into my pulse
and I bring my newly aromatic
joint to my face.

This was before I knew the name
of that heady scent spilling
from teacups filling cafés
in steam and clink of pastry plates.
Before how the smell of a big pot
of chicken soup cooking in my kitchen
changed. Before I knew how
perfumous desire was, before I knew
the whiff of missing a lover.

Zoo Animals

The Snow Leopard, the regal,
once illusive monster becomes
a freak show, family entertainment;
who'd have thought eating
flesh could excite so much.
But here, at feeding time,
caged out of his wild home,
taunted with crunchy children all day,
little scampering treats just out of reach,
his fat precise paws unable
to swipe through metal bars, unable
to attend to the scent

of fresh kill, we smell
his hunger and his sadness.

The sweating penguins airing their armpits
in their Cleopatra reed-lined pool.
The red-assed monkey clinging to its wired cage
pulling his butt hairs out.
The polar bear with skin allergies
gnawing on his arm.
The zoo holds its share of denizens
negotiating their language of pride.
You tried to hold my hand
at the gorilla compound;
I pulled away.
Even though I wanted
to put my arms monkey-like around you,
I haven't mastered the art
of publicly displaying affection.
I'd rather not have anyone see me;
one of our differences, the ability
to be looked at without flinching.

At the Insect Zoo
you squat on the floor
to ask the kid if he had ever seen
a Malayan beetle. *Yeah, they're everywhere
in summer,* he says; he lives in Petaluma,
little chance of sighting such an exotic insect.

I don't confuse the Californian and the Malayan
of the species, have stomped
on the latter in my slippers as a kid, delighting
in how they pop and splatter their bug juice.
But here, the targets of my childish cruelty
lay under glass, pinned and labeled and sprayed
with preservatives. Shiny exoskeleton,
scraggly clawed legs and hideous feelers
splayed and frozen for all time.
Would you dare hold it? the kid asks
and you grimace, illustrating your answer
with an exaggerated shiver.

I wanted to lean down and whisper
into your ear how easy it is to hold
that big ugly beetle in your loose fist
letting it tickle your palm:
the trick is to not squeeze,
to not mind its ugliness
and the smell it will leave on your palm.
It's the same trick to holding my hand.

The Only Living Man in the World
for David

In a world where every act must
be named and where every act has
no consequences, I can take
my man in my arms and smooch him
under the stars in the fog on top
of a hill overlooking the nightlights
of the city in which I love him
and call it a flowered cactus.
    He can tie me up and spit on me
in the act of love-making and I
will call it a yellow pearl. We
can devour all-you-can-eat rib dinners
all weekend and call it the drone of velvet.
We can delight in our isolation;

we can dodge the pinge of guilt or shame
or fear or boredom; we can be lovers
who return to a world to find friends
long gone, our homes burned to the ground,
our pets eaten, our families emigrated
to unpronounceable lands; we can burn
into each other's psyche like a brand
on the butt of a prized steer, we can get
high pissed drunk stay up all night
and get stinky in each other's arms
and I will call it
the reckless hiss of our life together.

    I tell you that if you should leave me,
my heart will turn to deep sleep and somewhere
I shall dream of acts that I cannot name
but in the darkness of my heart, and I shall
invent a language that sneaks your familiar,
your cherished body into the thorny terrain
of my blood. I will talk to barbed wire
and it will talk back to me.

Kirk Read

(1973 –

Kirk Read was born and raised in Lexington, Virginia, where he shattered his familiy's long tradition of attending Virginia Military Institute. He is the former editor of Our Own Community Press, *Virginia's award-winning queer monthly newspaper, and has a column appearing in a dozen gay periodicals. He lives in San Francisco.*

Blueberries

I promised myself that I wouldn't fall in love,
that it would be chill, under the radar and shit,
and here I go.
Boom goes the ax, plop goes me head.
So it's official.
After numerous attempts at being single,
autonomous, independent, alone,
I am a shivering pup again.
Against thousands of my own proclamations,
I let a 6'1, 190 lb 47 year old silver and balding
thick dicked Daddy with a moustache
fuck me into Thursday
and now am under the gently odd impression that it's love.
For me.
I know the guidelines of internet tricking,
perfectly evidenced when you said "I love you tonight."
After two hours in your grip I was almost able
to ignore that last word: tonight.
When erotic fantasies materialize full-blown,
it's a double therapy session waiting to happen.

When you held me down, your knees pinning my shoulders
I almost said "Stop."
Out came your mean streak—
ball gripping, nipple twisting horror of a man, grinning as I squirm.
Then, quietly, you reached for the metal spoon.
Fearing the worst, and admittedly not in the mood for a utensil beating,
I almost said the safe word.

But the spoon was for feeding, not hitting,
and you dipped it into a cup of blueberry yogurt,
careful to start me with half a spoonful.
With your free hand, you combed back my hair from scalp to tip,
running your thumb gently on my left temple.
So this is my favorite part of being kinky, eh,
when so many violent gulps of air have been chewed up
that all I can do is blow out a tiny stream of breath,
puppy eyes glazed over.
You raised the spoon a foot above my mouth,
releasing dollops of that lavender sludge onto my tongue.
I could die like this,
Daddy kneeling over me,
raking the edge of the spoon across my lips
to catch any missed drops.
And every time you say "Good boy"
And every time you say "Good boy"
And every time you say "Good boy"
I am the happiest boy that knees ever held in place.

White Hot

I think I'm ready to fall in love again.
The nights of wild impulse are over.
I've done my oat sowing and now I feel barren.
Like South Dakota.
You know you're ready to fall in love
when you feel like a Plains state.
I can see him in movies and books and strangers—
the lonely cowboy who smokes and cries
only occasionally
and wipes his feet twice before he steps into your house.
He's waiting for me
to kill the lonely part
and feed it to him with cinnamon
at dawn, before he steps into the sunrise.
He's waiting for me
to nuzzle his back while he shaves,
to spoon him to sleep
and adjust my breathing to his.

To ride shotgun closer than normal,
to allow him to smoke less and cry more,
to go to his Mama's church and sit in the third pew,
to help him paint fences
and irrigate the fields so they don't burn up.
And he wouldn't ignore me in the morning for some newspaper
and as he watched the evening news he'd hold me
and stroke my hair as the weatherman
predicted no rain, no rain.
And my mind wouldn't wander to other cowboys
as I lay beneath him.

We would shuck corn
and skin bucks
and shoe stallions
and hold hands
and laugh gently;
gather kindling
split wood, stack the pieces,
strike a match, set fire
to our hearth—
a fire that will consume everything around us
until all that we've built
is swallowed up by white hot flame so blinding
I can't imagine boredom
anymore.

Truck Stop Buddies

When I was 15
I'd take little thumb flick rides out to Lee-Hi truck stop.
It's not what you think.
I'd sit for hours on the vinyl bench seats of the lounge,
where standing ashtrays formed a maze
between the couches and the wide screen TV.
I told Shirley I was riding with my daddy,
which was true enough, if only in wish—
and I was so used to living in wish.
I think she figured me out on the 7th Saturday,
when there was still no father in sight.

The movies in the lounge
were always 80s blaxploitation movies like *Beverly Hills Cop.*
I never realized how entertaining black people were
to the hapless concubines of truckers.
I never heard the word nigger from a woman—just the boys.
Shirley and I split gravy covered french fries and watched NASCAR—
she was an Earnhardt fan and knew all the drivers.
She'd made her merry way through some of the pit crews
and told me which ones were drinkers
and which ones had sugar in their britches.
"A racer sure do break up the third shift," she'd say, mouth full of gravy.
Shirley had this habit of picking up fries,
eating half of them and putting them back on the plate.
So I knew to avoid the ones coated
with her signature shade of coral frost.
Shirley's definition of kindness was a man who'd drive 30 miles out of
his way to bop her at 2:30AM
en route to the Natural Bridge speedway.
My definition of kindness was a man who'd hold up his belly
so I could get to his stump without getting thwocked in the head.
Or, if he was born sweet, he'd give me a drag off his Kool
when I came up for air.
If I succeeded, that is, in resuscitating his shy and retreating peeter,
which was stubborn to rise
from a week of Vivarin, coffee, cigarettes,
and low-rent speed packaged as headache remedy.
Blowjob alchemy, turning 2 1/2 into 5 1/4 and hearing him say,
maybe as much as three times:
"You do good."

One day I was playing Ms. Pac Man,
about to turn over LARRY G's high score,
when a dirty thumbnail clicked two quarters onto the glass screen.
"Play ya," he said.
We played Ms. Pac Man for 39 minutes.
I finished 23 minutes after his last Ms. Pac Man expired.
I know this because I look at clocks compulsively,
and during that time I demolished this man named Jimmy
so thoroughly that I thought he, the vanquished,
might feel a compunction to conquer me in an extravideo activity.
I stared up at him as he shifted a duffel bag
from one shoulder to another.
"I'm a shower now," he said. "Thanks for the game."
I followed him into the shower and stood shivering in a neighboring stall.

Through the cracks of the curtains,
I saw Jimmy step out of the shower.
He stood at the sink, shaving.
I washed my hands, face, underarms, and even my feet in the sink.
Occasionally he'd catch my glance in a hand wiped hole in the mirror
and he'd smile and sorta scrunch up his cheeks at me.
After he wiped up, he looked around,
put his huge hand on the base of my skull,
and pulled me to his chest.
"Get on home," he said. "You're a good kid."
I can still feel his breath in my ear.

Finally I got my hands on some porn other than the copies of
Penthouse Letters, whose pages I mauled nightly.
A monograph entitled *Truck Stop Buddies* was among my acquisitions.
Reading it, I thought to myself "What am I doing wrong?"
How is it I got lost in Rockbridge County,
glaringly absent from the Rand McNally map of desire,
somewhere between storytelling and myth making,
undocumented sexual anthropology and wishful thinking.
Some boys apparently had the good fortune of being raped by coaches
and rescued from the streets by burly gentlemen
whose Buicks arrived just in the nick of time.
These kids got to be slave boys in Rome and arrested in Omaha.
I got to go to Vacation Bible School.
Well, I was 16 and I couldn't help feeling cheated.
Where in the world are all those 10-1/2 inch monster truck cocks
whose spit driven engines
can get through two states on a handful of saliva.
Where are those sloppy, at-first reluctant boyholes,
battered for a page and a half at a time
and yet mysteriously tight enough to render a firm, solid handshake.
Where are all the trucker daddies who pick up 3 local boys
on a slow day amidst diesel and doughnuts
and always brought one of them to the next stop?
That's the part of the story where I always shot.
I wanted to ride to the next stop.
"Don't let me go home a stranger" plays on the jukebox.
My RIDE TO LIVE t-shirt is folded and packed.
I have a toothbrush at the ready, a pocket knife
and a fistful of dime store dreams
and I'm still waiting
to ride to the next stop.

Permissions

All poems are copyright by the author unless otherwise stated.
All poems are printed by permission of the author or copyright holder.

Antler's "What Every Boy Knows" was first published in *The Son of the Male Muse* (Crossing Press, 1983); "Hot Summernight Cloudburst..." was fisrt published in *Erotic By Nature*; "On My Way to Lake Michigan..." first published in *Pennsylvania Review*; "For Blowjob Power" & "The Immortality of Boylove" first appeared in *Gay Sunshine* • "Boy wearing a dress" by Dan Bellm first appeared in *River Styx* (1996); "Boy wearing a dress" & "from Book of Maps" are from *Buried Treasure* © 1999 Roundhouse Press; "Transfigured" from *Buried Treasure* © 1999 by Cleveland State University Press • David Bergman's poems are from *Heroic Measures* by David Bergman (USU Press, 1998) • "Two Adams in a Sonoma Wood" & "Coming in for a Landing" are from *Special Deliveries* by James Broughton; "The Word for No is Yes" from *Hooplas* • "Picture of a Youth of Twenty-three" by Cavafy, translated by Ian Young, first appeared in *Gay Sunshine* • Justin Chin's poems are from his book *Bite Hard* (Manic D Press, 1997) • Ralph Chubb's work appears courtesy of Anthony Reid • Kirby Congdon's poems are from *Black Sun* (Pilot Press, 1973) & *Juggernaut* (Interim Books, 1966) both by Kirby Congdon • Dennis Cooper's poems are from *Idols* (SeaHorse Press) and *Boys I've Wanted* by Dennis Cooper • "Wife" & "Bodybuilder" are from *Wife* (Insight to Riot Press, 1993) & "Memoir" from *the red-heads* (Insight to Riot, 1997) both by Jim Cory • Gavin Dillard's poems are from *Yellow Snow* and *Satyriasis* by Gavin Dillard (Bhakti Books), several of them appeared first in *Between the Cracks* by Dillard (Daedalus, 1997) • "Turtle, Swan" is from *Turtle,Swan* by Mark Doty appears courtesy of David R Godine, Inc, © 1987 by Mark Doty; "The Death of Antinoüs" & "63rd Street Y" from *Bethlehem in Broad Daylight* by Mark Doty & appear courtesy of David R Godine, Inc, © 1991 by Mark Doty; "Homo Will Not Inherit" is from *Atlantis* by Mark Doty & appears courtesy HarperPerennial, © 1995 by Mark Doty • "Sonnet 1" by Robert Duncan, from *Roots and Branches*, © 1963 by Robert Duncan; "This Place Rumord to Have Been Sodom" by Robert Duncan from *The Opening of the Field,* © 1960 by Robert Duncan; "The Torso" by Robert Duncan from *Bending the Bow,* © 1968 by Robert Duncan; all Duncan's poems reprinted by permission of New Directions Publishing Corp. • "Dirty Old Man" is from *Counting Myself Lucky* by Ed Field (New Directions) and appears courtesy New Directions • Allen Ginsberg's poems from *Allen Ginsberg Collected Poems* (Harper Collins, Perennial Library, ©1984) appear courtesy Harper Collins & the Allen Ginsberg Trust • "Elegy", "Sweet Things" & "The Miracle" are from *Passages of Joy* by Thom Gunn (FSG, 1982) appear courtesy Farrar Straus Giroux; "Gift" first appeared in *Slate* • "me & ratboy..." was first published in *Chiron Review* (1997); "i'm not a punching bag", "what would Grandma think?" & "the club" are from *Ratboy, Etc.* by Michael Hathaway.(Kings Estate Press, 1994); "cinnamon man" from *stumbling into light* by Hathaway (Chiron Review Press,

1993) • Edward Lacey's poems appear courtesy of Fraser Sutherland • "How to be a hedonist" & "How to watch your brother die" were first published in *Poems for Lost and Un-Lost Boys* by Michael Lassell (Amelia, 1985); "Times Square Poems" first published in *Hanging Loose,* #50/51, Spring 1987; "Daddy" first published in *Decade Dance* by Michael Lassell (Alyson, 1990); "Dancer(s) with Dick(s)..." first published in *Eros in Boystown,* edited by Michael Lassell (Crown, 1995) • Timothy Liu's poems are from his books *Burnt Offerings* & *Say Goodnight* (Copper Canyon Press, 1995, 1998) • "Ode to Walt Whitman" is from *The Poetical Works of Federico Garcia Lorca, Volume I, Poet in New York,* Translated by Greg Simon and Steven F. White, Spanish text © 1940 by the Estate of Federico Garcia Lorca, translation © 1988 by the Estate of Federico Garcia Lorca, and Greg Simon and Steven F. White. Reprinted by permission of Farrar, Straus & Giroux Inc. • "Big Thick Dick" by Harold Norse first appeared in *Between the Cracks* (Daedalus, 1997); the rest were published in *Hotel Nirvana* (City Lights, 1974) and *Carnivorous Saint* (Gay Sunshine, 1977) • "Having a Coke with You" & "Homosexuality" are from *Selected Poems of Frank O'Hara* (Vintage, 1974) • "Second Sex Experiment" is from *Straight Hearts Delight* by Orlovsky/Ginsberg (Gay Sunshine Press) • Ian Young's/Marsha Shakley's translations of Sandro Penna first appeared in *Gay Sunshine* • Robert Peter's poems are from *What Dillinger Meant to Me* (SeaHorse, 1983) • Felice Picano's poems are from his collection *The Deformity Lover* (SeaHorse, 1978) • Vytautas Pliura's poems are from his book *Skating on the Dark Side of the Moon* (Alpha Beat Press, 1995); "Thomas" first appeared in *Chiron Review* • "A Muse", "Johnny Minotaur" & "Black is the Color..." are from *Some are Drowning* © 1994 Reginald Shepherd, reprinted by permission of the author and the University of Pittsburgh Press; "Eros in His Striped Blue Shirt" from *Angel, Interrupted* © 1996 Reginald Shepherd (University of Pittsburgh Press) • Adrian Stanford's poems are from his *Black and Queer* (Good Gay Poets Press, 1977) • Mutsuo Takahashi's poems reprinted from *A Bunch of Keys* by Mutsuo Takahashi © 1984 Hiroaki Sato, (The Crossing Press: Freedom, CA) • "Delphi," "The Gift of Dionysus," "Dream Creatures," "The Boy," "Pavane" are from *Pavane* (Sherwood Press, 1981); copyright 1981 by David Trinidad. "Love Poem" from *Answer Song* (High Risk Books, 1994); copyright 1994 by David Trinidad. • "Androgyne, Mon Amour" and "Winter Smoke Is Blue and Bitter" are from *Androgyne, Mon Amour* by Tennessee Williams (New Directions, 1977); "The Interior of the Pocket" from *In the Winter of Cities,* © 1951 by New Directions • "Given in Person Only" by Mark Wunderlich first appeared in *Quarterly West* • Ian Young's poems are from his books *Common-or-Garden Gods* (Catalyst, 1976) and *Sex Magick* (Stubblejumper, 1986).

Alphabetical Index